Cultural Identity of Tribes of North-East India

Cultural Identity of Tribes

of

North-East India

(Movement for Cultural Identity Among the Adis of Arunachal Pradesh)

Jagdish Lal Dawar

Head,

Dept. of History & Ethnography,

Mizoram Central University,

Aizawl

COMMONWEALTH

Cultural Identity of Tribes of North-East India

First Published : 2011

ISBN 81-7169-757-7

Published by :

Ajay Verma
For Commonwealth Publishers
4831/24, Prahlad Street,
Ansari Road, Darya Ganj,
New Delhi - 110002
Ph. : 3272541, 3257835
Fax : 91- 011- 3257835
e-mail : campusbooks@hotmail.com

Typesetting by :

Arjun Computers
Delhi - 110051

Printed at :
Roshan Offset Printers
Delhi

Preface

This book is the slightly revised version of the Project Report titled *Movements for Cultural Identity among the Tribes of Arunachal Pradesh since 1950's : A Case study of Aids*, submitted to the Indian Council of Historical Research, New Delhi. I am highly obliged to the authorities of ICHR for granting me the project.

Recalling the names of all who helped and assisted me in the preparation of this book is an almost impossible task; some are likely to be missed. The individuals and institutions I acknowledge below are just those that readily come to my mind; I beg the indulgence of others.

I am highly indebted to Prof. K.N. Panikkar who had supervised my Ph.D. work in Jawaharlal Nehru University and taught me the methods of historical research during 1981 - 1990. I am greateful to Prof. Bipan Chandra who provided me not only encouragement to pursue research but also valuable suggestions from time to time. I am grateful to Mr. Joram Begi, the former Registrar, Arunachal University and Prof. A.C. Bhagabati, the former Vice-Chancellor, Arunachal University for rendering me help whenever I approached them.

In fact, Prof. A.C. Bhagabati's name deserves special mention here since he provided me the anthropological tools for conducting field work and also clarifying and correcting many of my pre-conceived notions about tribal societies in general and of the tribes of Arunachal Pradesh in particular. I also acknowledge my thanks to Prof. Dwivedi, the Vice-

Chancellor of Arunachal University for reminding me all the time to finish the work in hand as soon as possible. I derive a sense of inspiration from his spirit in encouraging all the faculty members to engage in research activities. But I would be failing in my durties if I don't thank Prof. Tamo Mibang who initiated me into tribal studies. It is he who first of all advised me to do some research on the tribes of Arunachal Pradesh. I also thank Dr. Tai Nyori, the controller of Examinations, Arunachal University who is a prominent intellectual of the Adis and a eminent scholar and who has always been helping me in terms of providing the information not only on Adis but also on the other tribes of Arunachal Pradesh.

Besides I am indebted to large number of my friends and colleagues who had been source of inspiration in terms of discussion on various aspects of society. Some of these are : Bhagwan Josh, Manjit, S.V. Srinivas, N.C. Roy, P.K. Kuri, M.C. Behra, Deepak Mishra, A. Mitra, Sarit Chaudhury, Sucheta Sen Chaudhury, Tana Showren, Ashan Riddi, N.T. Rikam, Deepak Singh and Amarender Senger. I am specifically grateful to M.C. Behra who advised me to get the book published from Commonwealth Publishers.

I also thank the non-teaching staff of Arunachal University, particularly the Library Staff for providing me all types of assistance. I am also indebted to the staff of Nehru Memorial Centre for Contemporary Studies, Teen Murti House, New Delhi for rendering all types of help.

I am very grateful to my brothers Shri Roshan Lal Dawar, Shri O.P. Dawar and Mrs. Sneh Dawar (my sister-in-law) for helping me with secretarial work. Lastly, the entire credit of this book goes to my wife Smt. Usha Dawar, my daughters Shivali and Bhoomika who had to suffer a lot for not providing them sufficient time in domestic chores.

Whatever, the shortcoming left in this book the blame entirely goes to me.

Jagdish Lal Dawar

Contents

Glossary of Indigeneous Terms

1.	Abang	:	The sacred lores of the Adis.
2.	Apong	:	Adis' Rice beer.
3.	Bango Kebang	:	A Bango Kebang is one which all constituted with more than one village Kebang. Hence it is powerful.
4.	Bogum Bokang	:	It consists of more than one Bango.
5.	Dere	:	It is an Adi Community Hall in which all kinds of meetings are held, the young boys sleep at night and guests are received.
6.	Gangin	:	Temple.
7.	Gam	:	The village headman. In a village there are more than one gam, a social title for administration and social purposes. The most influential one is known as head gam.
8.	Kebang	:	The village council.
9.	Kadens	:	Friends.
10.	Miri	:	Traditional priest.
11.	Ponung	:	Dance.
12.	Mithun	:	An animal which was used by Adis as an exchange and also for sacrifice during festivals and other poojas.
13.	Nyibu Agoms	:	Sacred lores.
14.	Yaba	:	The Adi elderly people use 'Ya' in place of the first syllable of a girl's name to make it a pet name.

Chapter – 1
Introduction

Arunachal Pradesh is bounded by Bhutan on the West, Tibet and China on the North. On its South-East lies Burma whereas Assam stands on the southern boundary. Arunachal lies between 26° 28′ N and 29° 30′ N latitude and the longitude 91° 30′ E and 97° 30′ E. It covers an area of roughly 83,578 sq.kms. In 1961, its total population was 2,97,573. In 1971, 1981 and 1991 it was 4.68 lacs, 6.32 lacs and 8.65 lacs respectively.[1] It consists approximately of 26 major tribes and 110 sub-tribes and about 100 dialects (roughly).[2]

Historical Background - A Brief Outline

Before the British annexation of Assam in 1826, the Ahom rulers had followed a policy of appeasement to prevent the tribesmen from raiding the villages in the plains. The ahom rulers arranged some sort of subsidy called *Posa* to paid by some peasant families in cash or kind or both to the tribesmen. And if this policy failed to conciliate them punitive expeditions to punish the guilty hillmen were sent by the Ahom rulers.[3]

The British continued with the Ahom policy to frontier tribes with certain modifications in the payment of *Posa*. During Ahom rule the tribesmen collected their subsidies directly from the villages while the British officials made an agreement with the different tribes to collect *Posa* directly from the government. British also continued the policy of using military power in case of failure of the policy of conciliation.[4]

By the end of 1860's the British had evolved this policy

towards he frontier tribes of the North-East India which was essentially a policy of non-interference.[5] The introduction of Inner-line in the Lakhimpur and Darrang in September 1875 and March 1876 was basically an extension of the policy of non-interference.[6] However, as a result of developments in Lhasa in August, 1910, Chinese activities on the frontier and murder of Williamson, Assistant political officer, Sadiya in March 1911 at the hands of Abors, the British policy of non-interference was "replaced by a policy of loose political control."[7] According to D. P. Choudhury :

> The new policy had two distinct but inseparable aspects. On the one hand, the tribes were to be properly controlled, while on the other, the frontier was to be protected from any Chinese penetration or invasion. One without the other was impossible.[8]

The most important step in this regard was 'definition of Indo-Tibetan boundary.' And therefore, the Indo-Tibetan boundary took a final shape in 1914. It is known as Mac Mohan Line.[9]

In 1921, the Governor-General, acting under the Provisions of the Government of India Act of 1919, designated all the tribal areas of Assam as 'backward tracts.'[10] This regulation, "in effect, barred both the central Indian legislature and the Legislative Council of Assam from enacting legislation for the tribal areas without the express consent of the Governor-General or the Provincial Governor."[11] Thus while the north-east frontier tribal areas "were constitutionally a part of assam, the Government of Assam was denied a direct voice in the administration and governance of the area."[12] The Government of India Act of 1935, based on the recommendations of the Simon Commission, had done away with the terminology of Backward Tract and rechristened these areas as "Excluded Areas' and 'Partially excluded Areas."[13] The Balipara, Sadiya and Lakhimpur-Frontier tracts of NEFA were all designated as 'excluded areas.'[14] These were to be administered by the Governor of Assam under the general control of the Governor-General and with the assistance of an Adviser of Tribal areas and states.[15]

The question whether the Governor of Assam should be "allowed to retain his discretionery powers with regard to the tribal areas of the north-east India continued to be hotly debated in the Constituent Assembly which formulated and approved the Constitution of Independently India."[16] The Constituent Assembly of India had set up an Advisory committee on Fundamental rights, Minorities, Tribal and Excluded Areas under the chairmanship of Sardar Ballavbhai Patel.[17] For the North-East Frontier Tribal Areas and Assam Excluded and Partially Excluded Areas a sub-committee with five members was set up under the chairmanship of Gopinath Bordoloi, the then Chief Minister of Assam. (called Premiers at that time).[18] This sub-committee had submitted its report on July 28, 1947. Since the drafting of the constitution had already begun, the recommendations of the sub-committee were directly incorporated in the Draft Constitution.[19] Its recommendations were :

> We recommend that when the Central Government which now administers these areas (and which we consider it should continue to do with the Government of Assam as its agent) is of the view that the administration has been satisfactorily established over a sufficiently wide area, the Government of Assam should take over that area by the strength of a notification.[20]

The recommendation thus had two parts, namely : (1) Immediate replacement of the 'Governor' of Assam by the 'Government' of Assam as Agent to the Central Government'; (2) Full merger of the Frontier Tracts with Assam at a future date after administration had been fully installed over the whole area.[21] The first was realised by the India Provisional Constitution order of 1947, and remained effective until the position was reversed.[22] The second part was "never to come about as the political fortune and circumstances rapidly changed in the post-independently period."[23]

The 1950 Constitution virtually re-enacted the provisions of the Government of India Act 1935 as they applied to the excluded areas.[24] The other most important factor which possibly influenced the decision against direct extension of the Government of Assam to the Frontier Tracts was the emergence of Communist Government in China in 1949.[25] India's recognition of Tibet as an autonomous region of China had greatly changed the geo-political perspective of the international border in the north of the region.[26] The authority of the Governor of Assam acting in his discretion over the North-East Frontier Tracts as Agent to the Central Government was restored under the Constitution. A new and significant development was appointment of the external Affairs Ministry to act as the administrative agency for the President, and was, therefore, granted ultimate responsibility for the administration of this sensitive area.[27] On January 26, 1950, the adviser to the Governor of Assam assumed direct charge of the administration of the North-East Frontier Tracts, though his Secretariat was not separated from the Secretariat of the Tribal Affairs Department of the Government of Assam until June 1950.[28] After the separation, the civil servants of the Assam cadre were gradually replaced.[29]

The promulgation of the North-East Frontier (Administration) regulation, 1954, inaugurated a full-scale and integrated administration for the entire area under the designation of the North-East Frontier Agency-NEFA for short - for the first time.[30]

The constitutional separation of NEFA from Assam was finally brought about by the North-Eastern Areas (Reorganisation) Act of 1971 which converted it into a Union Territory under a Chief Commissioner.[31] Early in 1971," the Agency Council recommended a change of name in favour of 'Arunachal Pradesh' for NEFA against minor opposition from a section of NEFA students."[32] So NEFA came to be known as Arunachal Pradesh now-on-wards. It was declared a State in 1987.[33]

Cultural Zones of Arunachal Pradesh

Verrier Elwin divided the NEFA into three main cultural areas :[34] *(a)* People of western Kameng, namely Monpas and Sherdukpans who are inspired by Buddhist ideas.[35] They are to a "great extent under the influence of lamasery of Tawang."[36]

Both these tribes "combine in their religion and mythology traditional tribal ideas with the Buddhist theology."[37] In fairly close "geographical proximity live the Buguns (Khowas), Hrussos (Akas) and Dhammais (Mijis) who, although not Buddhists, share some aspects of their neighbours' cultures."[38] The Membas and other tribes living along the northern frontier may be conveniently grouped with them and so may be the Buddhist Khamptis and Singhphos.[39] *(b)* The central area is populated by a large number of tribal groups : Nishing (Daflas), Tagins, Hill Miris, Apa Tanis, Adis (Abors), Mishmis (Idu, Digaru and Miju). *(c)* The third group inhabiting the eastern Arunachal Pradesh is comprised of : Wanchos, Noctes and Tangsas. Noctes have "adopted a very elementary form of Vaishnavism."[40]

However, Parul Dutta and Syed Ishteaque Ahmad, the editors of volume XIV *Arunachal Pradesh* of the People of India Project have divided the cultural fabric of Arunachal Pradesh broadly into five cultural zones. These are : "*(a)* The Mon cultural zone, which covers the Tawang and Sherdukpens. The Akas, Mijis and Khowas also belong to this zone. *(b)* To the east of the first zone lies the Nishi cultural zone encompassing the Bangnis of the East Kameng district, the Nishis of the Lower and Upper Subansiri districts and two unique communities–the Sulungs and Apatanis. Other groups living in the zone include the Nas, Tagins, Mikirs and Hill Miris. *(c)* The Adi cultural zone extends from the eastern part of the Upper Subansiri district to the western boundary of the Dibang Valley district, covering all the Adi sub-groups as well as the Khambas, Membas and Mishings/Miris. *(d)* The Mishmi cultural zone, covering the districts of the Dibang Valley and Lohit, is predominated by the three groups of the Mishmi community, and among them lives a small community–the Zakhrings/ Meyors. Other communities in this zone are the Khamptis, Khamiyangs, Deories, Chakmas and Tibetans who are settled in the plains bordering Assam. In the past, the Khamptis and Khamiyangs have functioned as liaison between the Mishmis and people of Assam. *(e)* The nocte-Tangsa cultural zone is spread over the Tirap and Changlang districts. The major communities of this zone are the Noctes' Wanchos and Tangsas, with the Singhpos, Sonowal Kacharis, Lisus and Nepalis being the small groups inhabiting the area."[41]

Why is this difference between the two approaches, that is between Elwin and the editors of People of India series? Firstly, the two works were written during different periods, the former in 1958 and the later one in 1995. The Na tribe mentioned in the second cultural zone by the editors of people of India series was discovered in recent times. The Chakmas were settled in Arunachal Pradesh in 1964 and are given the status of refugees till today, so is true of Tibetans. The Nepalis were settled after Indo-China war and they are the descendants of the ex-soldiers and are not considered as the indigeneous group. The Lisus have not been recognized as the tribe by the Arunachal State Assembly. The Mikirs, Sonowal Kocharis and Deories are regarded as the tribes of Assam. Secondly, Verrier Elwin divided NEFA into three broader cultural areas on the basis of indigeneous beliefs and practices while the editors of the People of India series have not taken this into consideration and that seems to me the basis of discrepancy between the two authors.

The Adis

The tribes belonging to the central areas of Arunachal Pradesh : The Nishis, Tagins, Hill-Miris, Apatanis, Adis and Mishings (also in Assam) are grouped into Tani group of tribes. All of these tribes claim themselves as the direct descendants of their great legendary Human Father, called ABO TANI. The people of these tribes "are the ardent believers of a faith, called Donyi-Polo. By Donyi, they literally mean the Sun and Polo stands for the Moon. The conjugation of DONYI and the POLO becomes a strong channel of socio-cultural aspiration of the Tanis."[42]

The Adis, the subject of this study, constitute one of the major tribes of Arunachal Pradesh. They are found in the three Siang districts, *i.e.* East Siang, West Siang and Upper Siang, the eastern fringe of the Upper Subansiri and the South-western part of the Dibang valley districts. These areas lie, roughly speaking, between the subansiri river on the west and the Dibang valley on the east, Tibet on the north and parts of the districts of Lakhimpur and Dibrugarh of Assam in the South.[43] The Census of India, 1971 puts the number of Adis at 93,496 out of the total population of 4,69,511 of Arunachal Pradesh and thus they formed about 20% of the total population of the State.[44]

"The word Adi" says Elwin "covers a large number of tribal groups, united by a language that inspite of dialectical variations is fundamentally everywhere the same, and by a similar culture and temperament."[45] The Adis are divided into two broad groups : *(a)* Padam-Minyong group consisting of ten sub-tribes : the Minyongs, Padams, Pasis, Panggis, Milangs, Karkos, Shimongs, Tangams, Ashings and Boris;[46] *(b)* The Galo group comprised of four sub-tribes : Galos, Pailibos, Ramos and Bokars.[47] The two groups occupy almost two equal halves of the total area of the Adis. The rivers Sido and Siyom, roughly speaking, form the dividing line between the two groups, leaving the first group on the eastern and the second on the western halves.[48]

The Adis were known by the word 'Abors' earlier. The origin of the word 'Abor' has been interpreted variously.[49] According to one interpretation, it is Assamese in origin meaning savage, independent or hostile.[50] A second explanation is that "the name is an Assamese adaptation of an original Adi word which has since fallen into disuse."[51] A third interpretation is that it may have "some connection with Abo, the first man, according to Adi mythology, to whom they trace their origin."[52] The Assamese used the word in two senses. In the wider sense it meant independent, unruly, savage and so on, and as such it applied indefinitely to almost all the hill tribes on both sides of the Brahmaputra valley.[53] In its narower sense it meant particularly the hillmen living between the Subansiri and the Dibang. Today it is used only in the second sense.[54]

The Adis have dropped this nomenclature 'Abor' and prefer to be called as 'Adi' which in their own language, literally means 'hill' and thus in its extended and final sense 'the people living in the hills' or briefly hillmen'. Elwin says "they themselves have suggested and the administration has accepted, that they should be called Adis or hill men."[55] Its history goes back to the first Bogum Bokang Kebang held on 21st and 22nd March 1949 at Pangin village.[56] The leaders who organiased this Kebang were : late Kuttik Moyong, retired political Assistant, late Kep Taying Ex. Agriculture Inspector and late Tamik Dabi Ex Area base Superintendent.[57] In that "Bogum Bokang the issue of the use of the derogatory word Abor was discussed and a resolution was adopted to supplement the tribe name Abor with Adi which means the Hill-men."[58]

All the sub-groups, namely : Minyongs, Gallongs, Pasis, Padams, Milangs, Karkos, Simmongs, Boris, Bokars, Komkar, Ramo, Railipos, Ashings, Panggis, Tangams were "included in the general Adi banner."[59] The matter was referred to Administration of NEFA and was approved.[60] Since then, they have been mentioned as Adis in various records and research monographs.[61]. In a way it was the first important step towards forging of larger identity as well as cultural identity *vis-a-vis* the nomenclature provided by the 'other'.

REFERENCES

1. Census of India 1971, Series I, 1981, and 1991, Series I. The first census in Arunachal Pradesh was in 1961 but it does not figure in the main census books. It was done separately and I consulted this in Microfilm section of Nehru Memorial Museum and Library, Teen Murti House, New Delhi.
2. See the Census of 1971, 1981 and 1991, *op. cit.*
3. See G.D. S. Dunbar, 'Abors and Gallongs', *Memoirs of the Asiatic Society of Bengal,* vol. 5, pp. 15-16, cited in D. P. Chaudhury, *The North-East Frontier of India*, 1865-1914, The Asiatic Society, Kolkata, 1978, p. 29; E. Gait, *A History of Assam*, Kolkata, 1926, pp. 124, 126, 152-153, 157-58, 183; S. K. Bhuyan, *Anglo-Assamese Relations*, 1771-1826, Gauhati, 1949, pp. 31-34; A. Mackenzie, *History of the Relations of the Government with the Hill Tribes of the North-East Frontier of Bengal,* Kolkata, 1884, pp. 7, 21.

4. See. D. P. Chaudhury, *op. cit.* pp. 30-32.
5. *Ibid.*, p. 36.
6. *Ibid.*, pp. 37-41.
7. *Ibid.*, pp. 59-87.
8. *Ibid.*, p. 87.
9. *Ibid.*, pp. 114-160.
10. Leo E. Rose and Margaret W. Fisher, *The North-Eastern Frontier Agency of India*, Institute of International Studies, University of California, Berkeley, California, 1967, p. 22.
11. *Ibid.*
12. *Ibid.*
13. *Ibid.*
14. *Ibid.*
15. *Ibid.*
16. J. N. Chaudhury, *Arunachal through the Ages*, New Delhi, p. 235.
17. B. N. Bordoloi, 'Administration of Tribal Areas *vis-à-vis* the Sixth Schedule to the Constitution of India–the Founding Fathers' Views', *Vivekananda Patrika* (date and issue not mentioned), pp. 14-15.
18. *Ibid.*, p. 15.
19. *Ibid.*, p. 15.
20. Shibanikinkar Chaube, *Hill Politics in North-East India*, Quoted in J. N. Chaudhury, *op. cit.*, p. 234.
21. *Ibid.*, p. 234.
22. *Ibid.*
23. *Ibid.*
24. *Ibid.*, p. 235.
25. *Ibid.*, p. 235.
26. *Ibid.*, pp. 235-36.
27. *Ibid.*, p. 236.
28. *Ibid.*
29. *Ibid.*

30. *Ibid.*, p. 242.
31. *Ibid.*, p. 317.
32. *Ibid.*, p. 316.
33. Chandrika Singh, *Emergence of Aurnachal Pradesh as a State,* Delhi, 1989.
34. Verrier Elwin, *Myths of the North-East Frontier of India,* North-East Frontier Agency, Shillong, 1958, p. xiii.
35. West Kameng district has been further divided into two : West Kameng and Tawang.
36. Verrier Elwin, *op. cit.*, p. xiv.
37. *Ibid.*
38. *Ibid.*
39. *Ibid.*
40. *Ibid.* pxv; also see File No. 25, 1977-78 of Adi Cultural and Literary Society, Pasighat, p. 7.
41. K. S. Singh, General Editor, People of India, series, Parul Dutta and Syed Ishteaque Ahmad, eds., *Arunachal Pradesh,* Volume XIV, Anthropological Survey of India, Kolkata, 1995, pp. 20-21.
42. Oshong Ering, *Donyi-Polo – A Faith and Belief of The Tani,* Donyi-Polo Mission, Itanagar, Seires-1, p. 1.
43. Tai Nyori, *History and Culture of the Adis,* New Delhi, 1993, p. 1.
44. Census Report, 1971, Series-24, Arunachal Pradesh (District Census hand Book, Siang District) p. 19.
45. Verrier Elwin, *A Philosophy for NEFA,* Shillong, 1964, p. 18; Tai Nyori, *op. cit.*, p. 4; Sachin Roy, *Aspects of Padam and Minyong Culture,* NEFA, Shillong, 1966, pp. 11-12.
46. Tai Nyori, *op. cit.*, p. 4.
47. *Ibid.*
48. *Ibid.*
49. Verrier Elwin, *A Philosophy for NEFA, op. cit.*, p. 17; Tai Nyori, *op. cit.* p. 4; Sachin Roy, *op. cit.*, pp. 1-5; D. P. Chaudhury *op. cit.*, p. 12.
50. *Ibid.*

51. D. P. Chaudhury, *op. cit.*, p. 12.

52. *Ibid.*

53. *Ibid.*

54. *Ibid.*

55. Tai Nyori, *op. cit.*, p. 4; Elwin, *op. cit.*, p. 18.

56. Tanya Dabi, Secretary General Bogum Bokang Kebang, *Key Note Address* to Bogum Bokang Kebang on 19, 20th August 2000 at Rajiv Gandhi Stadium, Neharlagun, p. 2.

57. *Ibid.*

58. *Ibid.*

59. *Ibid.*

60. *Ibid.*

61. *Ibid.*

Chapter – 2
Nationalist Discourse and Cultural Hegemony in NEFA

I

During the 1950's the policy-makers of the Indian State had to grapple with the question of integration of NEFA with the Indian 'mainstream'.[1] The most important exponents of the formulation of this policy towards NEFA were : Sir Akbar Hydari and Jairamdas Daulatram (both of whom were Governors of Assam), N.K. Rustomji and K.L. Mehta (the two advisers to the Governor of Assam), Jawaharlal Nehru (the then Prime Minister of India) and Verrier Elwin, the adviser, Tribal Affairs to the Governor of Assam. However, Elwin played the key role since 1953 and largely moulded the Government's policy towards NEFA. The policy pursued in NEFA during this period is generally known as Nehru-Elwin policy. The cultural movement in Arunachal Pradesh will have to be understood in the light of discourse[2] provided by these policy makers. Movement for cultural identity is an important aspect of this cultural movement. The tenor of this discourse may be summed up in Elwin's words :

> Our policy is *to develop the tribe along the lines of their own tradition and genius.* The whole stress of NEFA policy is *on change.* We are all aware that very great changes, which we hope will be enriching rather than impoverishing, will come,

> but we would like to see these come, *not as imposed break with the past,* but by a natural evolution from it...There should be *no forcible imposition of another culture and...the old culture should be helped to grow and develop into the new.*[3]

In this respect the "minds of the people" must be diverted from "political issues to cultural pursuits."[4] It was believed to have "a political value." It was to "impress upon the people that we are not strangers, but can fit into the patterns of their own life."[5] The main purpose was to create a sense of legitimacy by filling the gap between "us" and "they." It would help "the local people and ourselves in one family with as little difference between us as possible."[6] In a nutshell the most effective method of integration was by way of exercising cultural hegemony.

The concept of cultural hegemony is associated with the work of Italian Marxist Antonio Gramsci, who developed his thoughts on this subject in *Prison Note Books* written between 1929 and 1935 during his incarceration in a fascist prison at Turi in Southern Italy.[7] The concept is related to the question of dominance and subordination in modern capitalist societies. A condition of hegemony exists when a 'fundamental social class' in 'the decisive nucleus of economic activity' exerts 'moral' and 'intellectual' leadership over both allied and subordinate social groups through the creation and perpetuation of legitimate symbols. The ruling group must also seek to win the consent of subordinate groups to the existing social order.[8] Hegemony simply requires that the subordinate be accomplices in perpetuating the symbolic structures that uphold existing inequalities.[9] In Arunachal Pradesh, the attempt to elicit the consent was made initially (especially upto 1962) by appropriating the tribal cultural practices.[10]

Culture is the site where the Indian State attempted to construct popular legitimacy and consent in NEFA. I am here, subscribing to Gramscian definition of the state :

> State is the entire complex of practical and theoretical activities with which the ruling class not only justifies and maintains its dominance but manages to win the active consent over whom it rules.[11]

The defining characteristic of the modern democratic State, according to Gramsci, is its educative and formative role. The State organises society on a broad front through practical, moral and intellectual 'leadership':

> Every state is ethical in as much as one of its most important functions is to raise the greet mass of the population to a particular cultural and moral level; a level (or type) which corresponds to the needs of the productive forces for development, and hence to the interests of the ruling classes. The school as a positive educative function, and the court as a repressive and negative educative function, are the most important state activities in this sense; but in reality, a multitude of other so-called private initiatives and activities tend to the same end–initiatives and activities which form the apparatus of the political and cultural hegemony of the ruling classses.[12]

II

The 'communist occupation of Tibet' and penetration of Christian missionaries from Assam to NEFA created a feeling among some of the political leaders that some strong steps would have to be taken to bring about "cultural and emotional integration of this area with the rest of the country."[13] After the Indian debacle in the Sino-Indian border conflict in 1962, and the demise of Nehru and Elwin in 1964, the so-called Nehru-Elwin policy was gradually abandoned. The exercise of cultural hegemony now takes a different direction. Now-on-wards the developmental programmes began to be introduced rapidly. In 1967 the North-East Frontier Agency Panchayat Raj Regulation was promulgated by the President of India. It was passed to be implemented in 1969.[14] Thus there was super-imposition of 'mainstream' political structure over her traditional autonomous socio-political institutions. It brought about series of changes in tribal polity.[15] Now-on wards less attention was paid to the appropriation of tribal culture and more on exercising the 'mainstream' cultural hegemony.[16]

III

STRATEGIES OF EXERCISING CULTURAL HEGEMONY

Though various strategies were adopted to exercise cultural hegemony I would be taking three aspects in detail. These are : (*a*) Education, (*b*) Architectural designs and (*c*) Popular culture.

III (a)

Education

Education is one of the important institutions through which the Indian State organized popular consent. Schooling was made as a means of moulding popular consciousness.

Priot to 1947 only two lower primary schools had been established in NEFA and both of these were located at the foot of the hills.[17] There are no census figures on literacy for NEFA earlier than 1961; "the best guess is that, as of 1950, there were only a few hundred literate tribesmen and that of these only a handful had been more than a primary education."[18] By 1961, literacy rate as shown in the Census of 1961 was only 2.3 percent among the tribal population of NEFA. A rapid expansion of education became one of the primary objectives of administration after 1950.[19]

The emphasis in the overall content of education was on national integration. Some illustrations from the policy document related to *Border Area Schools* would bring this point more clearly.[20] Stating the aims in Border Area schools, it was directed :

> It is proposed to rejuvenate the schools in the Border Areas and afford the children an opportunity for integrated education, thus bringing out all that is best in them. The other aims are to build up a feeling of self-respect and self-reliance, enlighten them as to what is great and good in our constitution, our history, our people, inculcate love for democratic living and develop in them the keenness to learn about the variety and sublimity of our culture, arts, philosophy, dress and languages.[21]

In the 'rejuvenation programme' the Time-table proposed for the Border Area Schools included :

The classes will begin every day with a common gathering of the staff and the students, where the following will be done after roll-call :

(i) A prayer in the local dialect (if such a prayer is in existence).

(ii) The pledge given below will be taken by all (this will be translated in the local language).

Pledge

'India is my country, all Indians in the hills or in the Plains, in the north or in the south, are my brothers and sisters.

'I love my country, and I am proud of its rich and varied heritage. I shall always strive to be worthy of it.

'I shall give my parents, teachers and all elders, respect and treat everyone with courtesy. I shall be kind to animals.

'I hereby take this solemn pledge that I will do everything possible to help to live in unity and shall consider all people of India as my own kith and kin, I shall be prepared to make any sacrifice and even lay down my life for the security and honour of my beloved country.[22]

Another important aspect of this Time-Table was :

'Before the dispersal of the students to their classes, they will sing full-throated, the National-Anthem which will be played and the students will be required to catch the correct tune. The meaning of the national Anthem shall be told in very simple language so as to drive home into their minds the value of the National Anthem. Emphasis should be laid on 'Himachala' clearly bringing out that the hills of NEFA are branches of the greater Himalayan range. The rivers of NEFA also merge in other great rivers of India and so the people of NEFA are included among the people of the areas mentioned in the National Anthem.[23]

One of the 'Extra-curricular activities was the conducted Tours :

> The students from the Border Areas must be taken on 'Bharat Darshan' tours, twice each year. One such occasion cold be the Republic day celebrations. These tours afford the students an opportunity of freely mixing with the students of other states, as also seeing for themselves the progress that India is making, and will inculcate a feeling of oneness.[24]

One of the Duties and Responsibility of a teacher in the Border Schools was "not only" to "instill in the child love for what is good and beautiful in his society but also for India and all people residing in it."[25] "Above all things," the teacher of the Border Area schools "should be patriotic in speech, thought and action."[26] He was supposed to be "thoroughly imbued with patriotic fervour so that he can inspire the students with the same spirit."[27]

The above discussion clearly brings out that education was utilised as a potent instrument for exercising nationalist hegemony over the people of NEFA.

III (b) (i)

Architectural Designs[28]

Architectural designs to be followed in the construction of public buildings (Government buildings, schools, hospitals, museums etc.) formed part of the exercising of cultural hegemony. It was agreed upon by the policy-makers to adapt "some of the attractive features of the local tribal constructions"[29] in the design of the public buildings. In the senior officers conference held in 1954 it was recommended :

> The architecture of the Educational Institutions should be adapted to the local pattern and some representation of the structural art of the local people should be made to fuse with the construction plan of our buildings, particularly, the school buildings.[30]

It was accepted in principle that building should "grow out of the landscape."[31] As Prime Minister himself pointed out "a building has to fit in with the surroundings and with the purpose in view."[32] The use of "brick and mortar" buildings was cautioned against because firstly, it was costlier and secondly these "do not fit in at all with their surroudings."[33] Moreover, it was believed that the cement houses and CIG roofs in villages would "create a gulf between our officers and the people."[34]

Before utilising the traditional architectural designs it was kept in mind the pattern was no to be uniform throughout NEFA. Since this region constitutes of heterogeneous cultures it was suggested that the designs were to be adapted taking into consideration the specificity of the cultural traditions of the tribe concerned. For example at Tezu it was decided to "use some Khamti temple design for the roof."[35] In the Siang district it was suggested to construct buildings along the lines of the *dere, moshup* or *bango* :

> Long buildings with hearths down the centre, raised on platforms, with a sitting platform at each end, and a small veranda all around.[36]

It was suggested by Elwin that "all school buildings" and also all other official buildings, "the floor will be raised off, the ground and will be made of bamboo in a style designed by official architects."[37]

Another important feature of the traditional houses is the sitting platform, "which is a very useful adjunct to any building as it enables the people to sit and warm themselves in the sun."[38] It was emphasised to incorporate this feature in the official buildings. "It would be useful even in front of a P.O's or A.P.O's bungalows."[39] It would serve a practical purpose besides adapting the traditional practice : "The tribal visitors would be quite happy to sit smoking or talking on it while waiting for an interview."[40] It was considered very essential for schools, hostels or staging-huts.[41]

Another important features of traditional architectural design is the practice of keeping a central fire-place. It was suggested to follow this pattern in the buildings to be constructed. As Superintendent Engineer in his note dated 30-6-60 to Elwin wrote :

> The existing policy is to provide central fire-places in buildings which will normally be used by tribal people, as they are accustomed to such type of fire-places.[42]

The introduction of central-hearths (fire-places) was given very importance. The policy-makers were aware that after having acquired modern education which is alien to the tribal traditions, the students may well become misfits in them :

> Students, whether in our schools or CITPC's, who live in hostels that are totally different from their own, will be less likely to return to their villages and may well become misfits in them.[43]

Therefore, in order to create the some environment as it exists in their homes, it was suggested to create central hearths in the school buildings, especially in the hostels, so that "the boys would feel at home" and "would be healthier."[44] It was tried in some of the inter-village schools.

III (b) (ii)

However, it was found that many of the tribal architectural adaptations which were utilised in *Bash type* buildings were not suitable in H. T. type buildings. Thus in a note dated 18-5-60 it is indicated :

> If we are going to have chairs, tables and beds in a room there is not much point in having the central hearth which does not fit in very well with the furniture.[45]

The note further clarifies how it was not possible from practical point of view :

> The buildings designed on the general plan of a Mishmi house do not work out very successfully in a HT building. The Mishmi house, with its low roof and six or eight small rooms, opening out of a corridor, is a very different thing from a building containing two rooms and a small veranda which is shut in by a low or high walls which does not come up to the roof.[46]

Therefore, the corridor was dropped from the plan.

Therefore, a process of selection, rejection and modification of the forms was involved to suit the altered conditions. Here the question of hygiene was given the utmost importance :

> The tribal houses themselves require some modifications because they do have a number of un-hygienic disadvantages which in the interest of health must be removed. We, therefore, must give attention to housing and here again evolve designs which would certainly retain the *existing attractive features* of the tribal Houses *but also suitably modify them to ensure that the layout lends itself to health.*[47]

The concern with modern conceptions of hygiene seems to be responsible for rejecting a few other elements too :

> The sitting platforms attached to schools and other buildings are most important, but the walls or railings surrounding them are not popular. In Tezu the boys hardly use the sitting platform and use walls or railings to hang up their linen to dry.[48]

Therefore it was suggested to give up any idea of surrounding these sitting platforms with walls or railings. In fact, the people were persuaded to "recondition their houses under hygienic conditions."[49]

The policy-makers' emphasis on the question of sanitation and health was governed by the modernist view of city. In this Dipesh Chakravarty's comments relating to the question of 'health' in pre-modern societies, seem to be relevant. He points out that when it comes to questions relating to 'health' the "pre-modern is always already condemned in our social science, however sympathetic the stance of our ethnography. As social scientists, we align ourselves with those who want to build citizen-cultures."[50]

While emphasizing on the importance of 'self-help' basis for creating a sense of legitimacy, it was also realized that it should be under the direction of administration :

> A school building constructed by the villages and maintained by them as their own, would make the people proud of their institution and also *help to wipe out the wrong impression that prevails in that Administration is forcing education on the people.* It was, therefore, decided as an experimental measure that the village schools will continue to be constructed either by the villagers on self-help basis or initially by NEFA Administration

> as OB type tribal constructions and that the future maintenance and renewal be left solely to the villagers.[51]
>
> However, it was also realized at the same time that :
>
> There is a tendency among the tribal people when asked to put up buildings on self-help to make them of very inferior specification with badly woven tarza walling, thin layers of thatching and on kutcha ground.[52]

The policy-makers attitude to buildings constructed by the tribals on self-help basis, evokes, at least, implicitly the image of modernity confronting a backward, static, and traditional society. This is implied in the following passage :

> The general quality of the buildings in the interior is deplorable and there must be a fantastic waste of public money in erecting at the cost of thousand of rupees these *miserable hovels in which our men are condemned to live*...Moreover, *the tribal people are having to build in a style they do not understand and accordingly do it badly.*[53]

It was, therefore, felt that if a teacher had to be provided in a village the following specifications were to be adhered to by the tribal people while carrying out the work on self-help:

(*a*) Strong change floor to be provided, raised 4 above ground.

(*b*) Tarza walls to be constructed according to their best and not their worst tradition.

(*c*) There should be *adequate light and ventilation.*

(*d*) Thatching should be properly done and tied down with bamboo jiffries. Thickness should not be less than 9.

(*e*) School compound should be of reasonable size and properly fenced.

"For the experiment to become a success, it will be necessary for the political officers and their staff to convince the villagers by intensive effort, of the psychological advantage of this new arrangement."[54]

III (b) (iii)

The improvement of the existing architectural designs was the hallmark of the policy. For this certain models of 'attractive houses' incorporating various tribal elements were designed by the architects.[55]

In fact improvement is the general policy in all aspects of the tribal economy and society. There was emphasis on the improvement of taste of the native public as regards beauty of form and finish in the articles of daily use among them. Their aesthetic judgement was of course wholly derived from Indian and European conceptions of beauty. Architectural designs formed part of this larger discourse of improvement, betterment or in other words, of overall developmental process. The categories of 'improvement', 'progress', 'inspiration', 'inducement' formed leitmotif of their writings. These words mean more than their literal meaning. It reveals attitudinal biases which were shaped by the 'modernisation' model.

Thus ATA (Adviser Tribal Affairs) felt that "the tribal people themselves should be made to improve their houses under the guidance of NEFA officers."[56] The remarks made by The Development Commissioner, NEFA, Shillong Colonel P. N. Luthra, as back as 1-3-57 are very revealing. He suggested more effective methods of exercising hegemony :

> We make some posters illustrating how houses can be imporved. For example, we could show somebody falling through a bamboo floor and side by side a nice plank floor with the housewife cleaning it with a broom. We could similarly show the interior of a house pitch-dark with children rubbing their eyes as result of the smoke and everyone looking very dirty and beside it in another interior showing a house with good windows and a chimney with everybody clean and bright-eyed children and so on. I suggest that this might be more effective method of achieving what we want.[57]

A not in Elwin papers states :

> It is important that when the NEFA people erect Basha type buildings on a self-help basis and of course always when they

> work on contract they should be induced to follow not what they have come to imagine to be appropriate for an official buildings, but the new specifications that we are now making.[58]

It was suggested to give "great importance to improve the technique of thatching throughout NEFA" and "every attempt" was "made to induce the people to improve the roofs."[59] It was also recommended to create the double roof system.[60] In case of use of CIG sheets it was advised to paint these in "a suitable green or dark red colour."[61] Because paint "preserves the sheet" and "adds enormously to the aesthetic appearance of administrative centres."[62] In case if the people buy CIG sheets at their own expense, "it might be made a rule that these should not be permitted unless they undertake to paint their roofs."[63]

The Adviser to the Governor put forward a point that "knowledge and experience gained in experimentation of new ideas must be utilised " in effecting changes in the construction of tribal houses by providing double roof, additional ventilation, separation of latrine blocks by passages etc." for future developments.[64]

In fact hegemony was also exercised in the sense of creating the model villages. Thus it was discussed at length that the CITPC (Cottage Industries Training cum Production Centre) might be planned as a model village.[65] The local style would have to be incorporated in these model villages but "the whole settlement planned in such a way that it would inspire not only the trainees but all tribal visitors with ideas about building and planned their own and villages."[66]

At another place, in a note dated 23-7-58 it is stated :

> The whole point of this is that the CITPC should be a model village and that the buildings should not be of the ordinary OB type put up by our own tribal contractors but that they should be real model tribal houses which would be an inspiration to the local people and to the trainees themselves.[67]

III (b) (iv)

What was the response of the tribal elites to these architectural designs? In fact, were not simply the passive recipient of these ideas. Thus Oshong Ering did not agree with Elwin's proposal to construct hearths (fire-places) in inter-village schools. In a D. O. Letter No. Do-1/60-61/dated 29th. September 1960 to Verrier Elwin he expressed his disagreement and dissatisfaction over this proposal. He wrote this letter after his visit to the Inter-village school, Sile in Pasighat division. He was shocked to see some hearths inside the hostel building of the institution. He protested against this decision on the grounds of (*a*) aesthetics, (*b*) Hygiene, (*c*) Tribal traditional practice, and (*d*) Discipline. According to him the construction of hearths violated all the above-mentioned norms. Moreover, he advocated that this was a new element :

> So far we know, hearths have not been constructed in Pasighat and Along High Schools. If small boys and girls can study in these high schools without having hearths, why boys and girls in inter-village school will not be able do the same.[68]

These grounds reveal how the elites had been hegemoniesd by means of education. What the letter speaks is the language of modernity, or civic consciousness, of health. It speaks of certain ideas of beauty, an order of aesthetics from which the ideals of public health and hygiene cannot be separated.[69] It is also the language of modernist nationalist. It speaks of liberal democratic construction of reality and it may also be the product of a particular kind of domination.[70] It reveals how effectively the culture of liberal democracy has been inculcated among the subjects.

To conclude this section : While conceiving themselves as participants in the on going traditions of tribal Architecture, the policy makers made an effort to hegemonise those traditions with the values of modernity and thus creating a space for national integration.

III (c)

Popular Culture

Another important site of exercising cultural hegemony was popular-culture. By the category 'popular-culture' we mean : the Press, film, radio and television. It is variously known as 'mass-culture', 'popular-culture', 'commercial-culture', 'culture-industry', 'popular-culture.'[71]

Writing on the impact of electronic media on the minds of the people R. K. Chatterjee points out :

> The electronic media such as radio, television and films affect the minds of the people so intimately that through them the people almost sense, as it were, a feeling of actual participation in national affairs.[72]

He further states :

> The activities of the mass-media follow closely the developments in various fields, informing people, reacting to policies and creating the social climate in which development and nation-building programmes can take place.[73]

We would take up for discussion radio, television, films (video-parlour houses) and press.

III (c) (i)

Radio

The radio had been an important instrument of exercising hegemony. Long back the Frankfurt School had stated it as part of 'an ideological state apparatus'. The medium of radio, Max Horkheimer and Theodore Adorno asserted in the 1940's, "turns all participants into listeners and authoritatively subjects them to broadcast programmes which are all exactly the same", resulting in "the stunting of the mass-media consumer's power of imagination and spontaneity. The might of industrial society is lodged in men's minds."[74]

In 1948, speaking in the Constituent Assembly, Jawaharlal Nehru had said that his "own view" of the AIR (All India Radio) set up was that it should "approximate as far as possible to the British model, the BBC." He visualised it to be semi-autonomous corporation under the Government. However, he then thought that it was not immediately feasible.[75]

The Vidyalankar committee had visualised the objectives of radio development in the post-colonial India :

> To inform, persuade and inspire, to make people's minds receptive, to familiarise them with social and material changes that planned development brings in its wake and to develop local initiative for decision-making.[76]

In fifties, radio for "promoting emotional understanding and integration of the country," was being visualised as a potent instrument. Therefore more attention was laid on the Rural educational programmes. In the fifties The All India Radio both its headquarters and its 31 stations aimed at providing education to the tribal and rural populations.[77]

> The Ranchi station situated in the heart of Chota Nagpur tribal area in the Bihar state, was inaugurated in 1957 mainly for programmes intended for these tribal groups and the nearby industrial labour. Likewise, at the Gauhati's station of All India Radio, there is a separate service meant for tribal and rural populations, which broadcast programmes in no less than 28 tribal languages practically al devoted to adult education in a broad sense.[78]

In 1957 there were 200,000 (2 lacs) radio sets in Indian villages and out of which 90,000 (ninety thousand) were of the 'community listening type.'[79] By 1971 the total number of "broadcasting stations in the country was 69 and the number of transmitters in operation 138. This is a considerable improvement over the position in 1947 when there were only half a dozen radio stations in the country and about a dozen transmitters with about 275,000 radio sets for the then population of 320 million people. At that time, less than 10 percent of the country was covered by radio facilities and less than 25 percent of the population as far as medium-wave broadcasting was concerned."[80]

In 1971 in Arunachal Pradesh there were two radio stations, that is, at Tezu and Pasighat. Besides, from the Dibrugarh station in Assam the programmes in tribal dialects Tangsa, Nocte, Idu-Mishmi, Wanchoo, Nishi, Adi, Apatani were being broadcasted.[81]

According to Subir Ghosh,

> The Government of India down to 1970, tended to set the electronic media as an instrument of Planning Commission,

the agency with the highest responsibility for implementing national development based on industrialisation.[82]

Radio and Tribal Development in NEFA

Arunachal (formerly knows as NEFA) was being administered from its headquarters at Shillong. Most of the District headquarters till late fifties had not yet been linked by roads. In order to maintain links with the staff serving in distant frontiers a programme of a 'series of broadcast talks was inaugurated by N.K. Rustomji Advisor to the Governor of Assam, on 15th August, 1959. It became a weekly newsletter and was broadcast on every Sunday afternoon. Stating the objective of this broadcast N.K. Rustomji remarked :

> Our idea has been that as one large family and united family, we should keep our various members scattered in far-distant outposts, continually in touch with each other.[83]

He further stated :

> I have mentioned on many occasions that these broadcasts are not intended to be as "sermons from the Mount," but rather in the nature of talks to our family members, as we might talk together over a cup of tea or a *chunga* of zu.[84]

Ostensibly these weekly broadcasts were meant for the officials of NEFA but planners sitting at Shillong were very well aware of the fact these were also being listened to by the indigeneous leaders. Especially when the concept of 'community listeners' was being floated and radios for communities were being provided in rural areas, these broadcasts must have been leaving some impact on the indigeneous population. The officials were concerned to disseminate their developmental programmes to the tribals. Thus in a broadcast on October 16, 1960, the focus was on the report of speech delivered by the Adviser N. K. Rustomji on the occasion of inauguration of first Census Conference of Division Statistical officers on October 12, 1960 :

> Speaking on the occasion the Adviser stressed the importance of collecting accurate and complete information regarding NEFA population, as it will be vitally important for our development plans and other administrative policies. He

> stressed that this could be achieved only if there is full and active cooperation of both officials and the people. He struck a note of caution against spreading rumours as to our purpose. In fact we should make the people quite certain as to what we are after. This will alone enlist active and positive support of the people instead of just their allowing us to count them.[85]

One of these broadcasts was in the form of a radio-talk (2 ½ minutes) on the question and answer form. K.L. Mehta, adviser to the Governor of Assam replies on the question regarding the progress in extending and consolidating administration in North-East Frontier Agency :

> ...All the same we have opened several administrative centres right up on our borders, where officers stay on a permanent basis and help the tribal people to increase their production, to take better care of their health and to derive the benefits of education.[86]

And then to the question 'what progress has been achieved in the development of these areas'? Mehta replies :

> We have no law and order problem to speak of and development of the region is taking place along the lines of local traditions and genius.[87]

To Elwin the question was put "what has been the impact of the new administration on the people in the interior and how are they reacting to it"? Elwin replied :

> It has been unexpectedly favourable. Until fairly recently, there were great areas where you couldn't go without a military escort; sometimes the people would hide in the jungle; they had no idea what India was.
>
> Now all that is changed. I myself have toured in some of the remotest areas, always without escort, and everywhere I have found friendliness, hospitality and a growing love of India. The people specially appreciate three things : the first is the peaceful life introduced among them; the second is the removal of certain forms of exploitation of weaker by stronger groups; and the third is the attitude of the officers who come to them as friends and brothers, imposing nothing on them, regarding their way of life while trying to save them from the bad.

> The result has been that the people have responded enthusiastically : they are coming to our hospitals, sending their children to school, taking to wet-rice cultivation and so on. At the same time, there are signs of a revival of tribal culture. Where weaving had died, the women are returning to the loom; they dance and sing more, not less than they did. There is much more happiness in these frontier hills than there had ever been before.
>
> The thing may be summed up in what an old slave woman said to me when she was liberated. "For years I travelled below the ground in darkness, but now I have come into the light of the sun.[88]

III (c) (ii)

Post Indo-China War and Mass Media

The Mass-media faced a new challenge in the post Indo-China war period. The planners had to take new steps to check the hostile propaganda on the part of the Chinese, especially in the border areas. R.K. Chatterjee in his book *Mass Communication* throws some light on this aspect :

> . . .the biggest problem of mass communication was posed in the Himalayan border areas of the country where for centuries people had lived in isolation from the plains of India and had had traditional intercourse with the people of China. Thus, along with the helping in the arrangements for creating a popular front in the border areas, mass communication had to take the task of integration of the border people in the national stream. The present-day China and India represent two different schools of political thought. People in the border areas were the direct victims of hostile propaganda. The free and democratic way of life obtaining in India had to be presented to them.[89]

III (c) (iii)

Television

The television in India was introduced on 15 September, 1959 on an experimental basis in the form of a UNESCO's pilot project.[90] Its object was "to study the use of TV as a medium of education, rural upliftment and community development".[91] Another project of school TV programme was undertaken in 1961.[92] From Independent Day of 1965, "commenced" a regular TV service in India for one hour duration. Since that day TV has come to stay in India.[93] Enumerating the growth of TV since 1970 Ronald Inden in a recent article writes :

> "There were only 22, 000 (Twenty two thousand) T.V.'s in India in 1970, all imported : There are now estimated to be around 65 million TV households in India (more than in France and Germany combined), three-fourths of which are in small towns and villages."[94]

Citing Keval Kumar Inden aserts.

> The number of people watching TV has gone up dramatically. By 1991-92 some 175 million people (140 million urban, 35 million rural) were watching in 35 million television sets on a daily basis.[95]

Therefore, he concluded "India now does have something like a modern, mass society."[96]

Forging of National integration has been one of the foremost objective of Television from the very beginning. In a seminar organised by All India Radio in 1973 objectives of T.V. spelt out were :

(1) Television must be utilised as aid in the developmental process and as an instrument of social change and national cohesion.

(2) Special emphasis is being laid on using cultural programmes to foster national pride and national integration instead of providing merely popular commercial or revenue earning programmes.[97]

Long after the proliferation of private - satellite channels it was still stated by the Minister of Information and Broadcasting in 1995-96 that D.D's "main aim is national integration, inculcating a sense of unity and making people proud that they are Indians."[98]

During my fieldwork conducted in the areas of my study I made a survey of the nature of impact of Television viewing on the indigeneous people. I found that Hindi films were very popular among the people. Till late DD I and Metro were the only channels telecast on TV in Arunachal Pradesh. The private channels got entry very recently. Therefore people had no option but to watch only D.D's programmes.

III (c) (iv)

V.C.R. Technology

Another technology which really popularised the Hindi Cinema was the diffusion of video technology. V. C. R's started to "diffuse rapidly after the Asian Games in 1982, when Doordarshan's black-&-white television broadcasting went coloured, and when the Indian Government liberalized import duties on T. V. sets."[99]

III (c) (v)

Video-Houses & Films[100]

A few cinema-houses had been opened in Arunachal Pradesh in late 60's and early 70's but the Video-Cinema was introduced in 1983. Since then it became very popular and large number of video-licences have been issued by the Directorate of Information and Publicity, Government of Arunachal Pradesh. Thus the figure upto 21-5-96 is :

(*a*) Video-Lincences : 717.

(*b*) Cinema-Hall Licences : 63.

A survey conducted during my field work brings out the fact that the video-houses were very popular in the different parts of Siang valley. Even the proliferation of private channels telecasting large number of Hindi films has not decreased the popularity of Video-houses. One of the reasons being the experience of watching films in the video-house where large number of viewers sit together and watching the film creates a sort of community. In a way it is an important aspect of leisure activity. Secondly, in most of the small towns power-supply is erratic and that too for a very limited period. The video-houses have their own small scale power generators. This makes the popularity of video-houses in small urban centres. I conducted interview of cross-sections of viewers of different age groups, gender, social, educational and economic backgrounds. An analysis of these interviews has brought out an important fact to me that Hindi Cinema has played an important part in exercising nationalist hegemony in terms of law, language and taste among the people of Arunachal Pradesh. It is therefore, worthwhile to discuss it in a bit detail.

III (c) (vi)

In order to define problems of the film industry and to suggest means of removing them, the Government of India set up The Film Enquiry Committee in 1950. One of the three aims stated by the committee was to examine what measures should be adopted to 'enable films in India to develop into an effective instrument for the promotion of national culture, education and healthy environment."[101] "Representatives of the Government," says Sumita Chakravarty, "stressed the socially useful role that the cinema could play, its importance as an educational and uniting force in the nation, and its ability to project India's economic development before its audience."[102]

Therefore, the two differing aims of 'entertainment' and 'education' were simultaneously stressed. In a way these two differing aims performed the same function, that of exercising hegemony. The central thrust of entertainment is 'utopianism'; that is, it projects imaginary solutions to real problems as the only available ones. As Richard Dyer point out :

> Entertainment offers the image of 'something better' to escape into, or something we want deeply that our day-to-day lives don't provide. Alternatives, hopes, wishes – these are the stuff of utopia, the sense that things could be better, that something other than what it can be imagined and may be realized.[103]

The creation of utopia among the film-goers is evident the way two of our respondents replied to the questions 'what constitutes a good film? or 'what type of films you like most'? A good film is one which represents stupendous efforts of a person to achieve 'greatness'. By 'greatness' he meant a rich person who saves lot of money and constructs a big house. A desire to own big houses similar to the ones represented in the Hindi films was expressed by another respondent also. These are real needs created by the capitalist society. That is, while entertainment "is responding to needs that are real, at the same time it is also defining and delimiting what constitutes the legitimate needs of people in this society."[104]

One of the important institutions that symbolises State power, especially in the popular consciousness, is the law. Here 'popular consent' is organised as a social and political force. Cinema has been an important site to build consensus on the issue of law-and-order. It is an hegemonic project. This is explicit in the way our respondents reacted to the question of representation of terrorism in films and also their liking for films invoking patriotism. The popularity of the film "Hakikat' representing war between China and India and the way it had been able to 'interpellate' most of our respondents is a good example of Cinema as an ideological form. Althusser calls the process by which ideology 'grabs' people 'interpellation'. "All ideology hails or interpellate concrete individuals as concrete subjects."[105] Interpellation is like someone calling out, "Hey, you there" in the street. When the hailed individual turns round, "by this mere one-hundred and eighty - degree - physical conversion, be becomes a subject.[106] The person imagines the call is directed to him/her personally, and by reacting, becomes subject to it and to the person calling out. Interpellation explains how the lure of film narrative unconsciously gathers viewers into the value-system, beliefs and ideology of the narrator. Therefore, entertainment/ pleasure is not just a private and personal affair but inextricably bound up with questions of social order. The identification of our respondents with the heroic battle of Indian army consisting of a few solidiers with huge Chinese army was able to engender empathy. Thus pleasure and identification play strategic roles in the reproduction of certain values,107 here the values of patriotism. Pleasure, therefore, is a key political and ideological issue.

This film 'Hakikat' created a desire in one of our respondents to 'serve the nation.' Another respondent averred "It is natural to shed tears for the nation after seeing 'patriotic' films like 'Hakikat.'" Such films, would 'foster national integration' asserted a respondent. He believes "Arunachalis are more patriotic than any Indian elsewhere." For another respondent, patriotism meant : (*a*) 'The whole of Hindustan is one'; (*b*) 'terrorism is bad.' He believes terrorism is abetted and supported by Pakistan. He gave the example of terrorism in Pubjab and Kashmir. In fact he abhors terrorism. He developed "these views after watching Hindi films."

The Bombay Cinema thus has been an important site of creating an awareness of the 'imaginary' unity of Indians and the Indian nation state. Here Benedict Anderson's statement about the 'nation' as 'an imagined political community' may be cited :

> Nation is an imagined political community...because members of even the smallest nation will never know most of their fellow-members, meet them, or even hear of them, yet in the minds of each lives the image of their communion.[108]

The 'nation' as 'imagined community' is also implicit in the views expressed by most of our respondents on an important aspect of 'educative role' of Bombay Cinema, that is 'learning' about the various places in India, (say *Mumbai, Delhi, Khandala, Madras, Bangalore* etc.). That is, one forms ideas about the geography of India. "The Hindi Cinema" from its earliest days" Sumita Chakravarty tells us, "used the image of map in interpellating viewers in all their diversity as unified national subjects."[109] Foucault has drawn our attention to the idea of history-geography as 'constitutive of' a 'national discourse' and also of 'implanting and inculcating the civic and patriotic spirit."[110] He also traces the history of "map as instrument of power/knowledge" in western society.

The building of the consensus on the issue of law and order is further extended in the symbolic order of the father. Here Sumita Chakravarty's observation is significant :

> In order to give a concrete shape and presence to 'the nation', in order, that is, to make it a myth, the Bombay film invested the law, representative of the nation, with the moral authority that inheres in a parent.[111]

Our respondents asserted that Hindi films are good because these teach obedience to father and the elders. A wife can learn how to pay respects to her husband.

III (c) (vii)

Another important site of exercising of cultural hegemony is the realm of taste. It is a site of 'contestation and cultural domination'.[112] Raymond Williams has surveyed the historical trajectory of the meanings of the word 'taste' in the English language.[113] He notes that, in the physical sense, the word 'taste' has been operative in the English language since the thirteenth century.[114] In the fifteenth century it was understood in the wider sense of good taste meaning 'good understanding.'[115] In the seventeenth century and early eighteenth the word 'taste' became equivalent to discrimination.[116] Taste has become, in other words, a 'power of the mind' identifiable to and acknowledged by a *community of taste* which recognizes certain criteria for the establishment of 'good' and 'bad' taste. Concluding his survey Raymond Williams notes :

> the idea of taste cannot now be separated from the idea of *the consumer*;...The two ideas, in their modern from have developed together and responses to *Art* and *Literature*...have been profoundly affected...by the assumption that the *viewer*, spectator and reader is a *consumer*, exercising and subsequently showing his taste.[117]

That the Bombay Cinema has been instrumental in promoting new tastes in terms of food, conversation, etiquettes, table manners, morals, dress, fashions etc, was corroborated by most of our respondents. One of our respondent perceives attitudinal changes among the Cinema-goers, especially the girls, who want to be now more 'sophisticated.' A student of Class XII of Hr. Secondary School, Pasighat informed us that the students generally, discuss about the moral message of the films over dining tables in the mess.

The ideas of 'cleanliness', 'hygiene', 'moral and physical improvement' etc. are related to the civilising discourse.[118] Pierre Bourdieu has argued that the apparently superficial reformation of manners is in fact one of the most powerful ways in which a culture inculcates its metaphysical, moral and physical scheme of things.[119] Thus the Bombay Cinema has created a new cultural 'commonsense.'[120]

III (c) (viii)

Language is one of the principal symbolic systems through which cultural hegemony is constructed. It is one of the codes of securing ideological domination.[121] Language, as Roland Barthes has observed :

> Fights for hegemony; if power is on its side, it spreads everywhere in the general and daily occurrences of social life, it becomes doxa, nature.[122]

It is an arena of class struggle, a struggle to win or resist hegemony.[123]

The Mumbai Cinema has been playing a very important role in popularising Hindi as the national language, especially in Arunachal Pradesh. One of our respondents stated that he learnt Hindi language mainly through watching Hindi films and now he enjoys watching films only in the Hindi language.

REFERENCES

1. The category 'Mainstream' recurs in the official papers that I consulted. However it is not defined. We can provide its definition from the perspective of an intellectual from the North-East India which at least would reflect the vernacular voice. Pradip Phanjoubam, an intellectual from Manipur in a seminar on 'Dynamics of Identity and inter-group relations in North-East India' held at The Indian Institute of Advanced Study, Shimla from 12 November to 14 November, 1996 states that 'various attempts have been made to define what constitutes the Indian mainstream" but "no conscretised definition has so far been forwarded." Pradip puts forward his definition as follows :

"The Indian mainstream is a stream that has its source in the obscure proto-historical period, a stream that began taking shape about 5000 years ago in and around the Indus Valley and flowed down the open Gangetic plains and emptied into the Bay of Bengal. Its influence however reached far and beyond just its basins, covering the entire sub-continent. The consciousness of being part of this historical stream is what is broadly the 'mainstream', in the Indian context. The mainstream history text books prescribed for schools and colleges will bear testimony to this."

—see Kailash S. Aggarwal, *ed., Dynamics of Identity and Intergroup Relations in North-East India*. Indian Institute of Advanced Study, Shimla, 1999, p. 139.

2. My use of concept of discourse is influenced by Hayden White, *Tropics of Discourse : Essays in Cultural Criticism*, Baltimore, 1978, p. 4.
3. Elwin Papers, File No. ATA/G/55, Secret, serialised as (listed as) File No. 96, p. 2. In manuscript section of the Nehru Memorial Centre for Contemporary Studies, Teen Murti House, New Delhi. (Now-on-wards it would be mentioned as only File No.) *Emphasis mine;* also see Nehru's Note on His Tour of the North-Eastern Frontier Areas in October, 1952, p. 5.
4. Elwin's note dated 28-12-58 in Elwin's papers, File No. ATA/G/4, listed as file No. 47, p. 72.
5. Elwin papers, File No. ATA/G/4, listed as file no. 47, p. 72.
6. *Ibid.*
7. Antonio Gramsci, *Selections From The Prison Note Books*, edited and translated by Quintin Hoare and Geoffrey Nowell Smith (International Publishers, New York, 1971), pp. 12-13, 53, 55-60, 238-39, 261-64; Antonio Gramsci, *Selections From Cultural Writings*, ed. David Forges and Geoffrey Nowel Smith, translated by William Boel Hower (Harvard University Press, Massachusetts, 1985), pp. 164-65, 172-73, 220-21, 342-43.
8. Antonio Gramsci, *Selections From The Prison Note Books*, pp. 55-60; Walter L. Adamson, *Hegemony and Revolution : A Study of Antonio Gramsci's Political and Cultural Theory* Berkeley and Los Angels; 1980), Ch. 6, pp. especially 170, 173; and Perry

Anderson, 'The Antnomies of Antonio Gramsci', *New Left Review,* 100 (1976-77) : 5-78.

9. T. J. Jackson Lears, 'The Concept of Cultural Hegemony : Problems and Possibilities', *The American Historical Review,* Vol. 90, No. 3, June, 1985, pp. 573-78.
10. For the concept 'culture as appropriation' see Roger Chartier, 'Culture as Appropriation : Popular Cultural Uses in Early Modern France', in Steven L. Kaplan, ed. *Understanding Popular Culture : Europe from the middle Ages to the Nineteenth Century,* Berlin, Mouton Publishers, 1984, pp. 229-33.
11. Antonio Gramsci, *Selections From The Prison Note Books, op. cit.,* p. 244.
12. *Ibid.,* p. 258.
13. B. Keskar, Minister, Information & Broadcasting, India to Jawahar Lal Nehru, The Prime Minister, confidential letter No. 34-S/61-M. O. dated Feb, 1961 in Elwin Papers, File No. 153, p. 15.
14. Regulation 3 of 1967 in P. N. Luthra, *Constitutional and Administrative Growth of the North-East Frontier Agency,* Shillong, 1971, Appendices, p. 123.
15. See Atul Chandra Talukdar, *Political Transition in the Grass roots in Tribal India,* Delhi, 1987, pp. 91-159.
16. See Jagdish Lal Dawar, 'Movement for Cultural Identity since 1950 among the Mishmis of Arunachal Pradesh', *Proceedings of North-East India History Association,* Silchar, 1995, pp. 322-23.
17. Leo E. Rose and Margaret W. Fisher, *The North-East Frontier Agency of India,* Institute of International Studies, University of California, Berkeley, California, 1967, p. 43.
18. *Ibid.,* p. 43.
19. *Ibid.,* p. 44; also see *Techno-Economic Survey of NEFA,* National Council of Applied Economic Research, New Delhi, December, 1967, pp. 112-122.
20. See Directive No. Ed. 3/113/61 in Verrier Elwin, B. Shastri and I. Simon, eds., *Important Directives on Administration of NEFA,* North-East Frontier Agency Administration, Shillong, 1967, pp. 164-169.
21. *Ibid.,* p. 164.

22. *Ibid.*, p. 166.
23. *Ibid.*, p. 167.
24. *Ibid.*, p. 168.
25. *Ibid.*, p. 169.
26. *Ibid.*, p. 169.
27. *Ibid.*, p. 169.
28. This section is a thoroughly revised version of the paper presented at the Fourteenth session of the North-East India History Association held at Jorhat in 1993 and published in its Proceedings, pp. 248-258. However, I have included more material in this section which I collected as a part of the grant given by I.C.H.R. for this study.
29. Note dated 19-7-55 by Colonel P. N. Luthra, Development Commissioner, NEFA, Shillong, in Elwin papers, File No. 47, p. 2.
30. P. N. Luthra to Superintendent Engineer, NEFA Letter No. Ed. 12/54/47, 12th July 1955 in Elwin Papers, *ibid.*, p. 2.
31. Elwin papers, File No. ATA/G/42, p. 18.
32. Prime Minister of India to the Chief Minister of Assam, copy of letter No. 496-PMO/59 dated Ist. August, 1959, in Elwin Papers, File No. ATA/G/42 serialised as File No. 73, p. 14.
33. Copy of the Prime Minister's Note dated 25-5-55 in Elwin Papers, *ibid.*, p. 16
34. *Ibid.*, p. 19.
35. *Ibid.*, File No. ATA/G/4, p. 94.
36. *Ibid.*, p. 31.
37. Note dated 15-3-58, File No. ATA/G/4, p. 33.
38. *Ibid.*, p. 19.
39. *Ibid.*
40. *Ibid.*
41. *Ibid.*
42. *Ibid.*, p. 96.
43. *Ibid.*, p. 26.
44. *Ibid.*, p. 31.

45. *Ibid.*, p. 91.
46. *Ibid.*
47. P.N. Luthra's comments dated 19-7-55 on the various paragraphs of the note by ATA. File No. ATA/G/4, p. 2. Emphasis mine.
48. File No. *ibid.*, p. 91.
49. *Ibid.*, p. 50.
50. Dipesh Chakravarty, 'Of Garbage, modernity and the Citizen's Gaze', *Economic and Political Weekly*, March 7-14. 1992, p. 542.
51. Minutes of the Meeting held in A. G's (Adviser to Governor) Room on the 22nd April 1960 in Elwin Papers, File No. *Ibid.*, p. 89, emphasis mine.
52. *Ibid.*
53. File No. *ibid.*, p. 19. Emphasis mine.
54. *Ibid.*
55. *Ibid.*, pp. 26-27.
56. See minutes of the Meeting Held in A.G's Room on the 22nd April 1960, *op. cit.*, p. 90.
57. File No. ATA/G/4.
58. *Ibid.*, p. 29.

    In the Elwin Papers I came across a note titled 'Architecture in Tirap' but it has not been signed any one. The date on this noting is not indicated. But it must be before 15th May 1958, because the note in question is paginated as No. 19 while a letter on p. 32 of this file is dated 15th May, 1958. In this note (p. 19) the writer is shocked to find "the deplorable" quality of the buildings in the interior areas. He seems to be doubtful whether the tribals would be able to construct buildings meant for the use of others, *unless they are trained.* (emphasis mine).
59. Elwin Papers, File No. ATA/G/4, p. 28.
60. Elwin's note dated 4-5-60, File No. ATA/G/42, p. 53.
61. File No. ATA/G/4, p. 28.
62. File No. ATA/G/42, p. 53.
63. File No. ATA/G/4, p. 28.

64. Minutes of the meeting held in A.G's room on the 22nd April 1960, File No. *ibid.*, p. 90.

65. File No. *ibid.*, p. 56

66. *Ibid.*

67. *Ibid.*, (23-7-58).

68. Elwin papers, File No. ATA/Cor/19, listed as File No. 39, p. 26.

69. See Dipesh Chakravarty, *op.cit.*, also Paul Rabinow, *French Modern : Norms and Forms of the Social Environment.* Cambridge, Mass, 1989, pp. 30-34; Peter Stallybrass and Allon White, *The Politics and Poetics of Transgression*, London, 1986.

70. See Douglas E. Hayes, *Rhetoric and Ritual in Colonial India*, The Shaping of Public Culture in Surat City, 1852-1928, Oxford University Press, 1992 p. viii (Preface).

71. See Fredric Jameson, 'Reification and Utopia in Mass Culture' in Fredric Jameson, *Signature of Visible*, Durham, 1989, p. 9; Theodor W. *Adorno* and Max Horkheimer, *Dialectic of Enlightenment*, Mr. John Cumming, NLB, London, 1979, pp. 120-167; Roger M. Keesing, 'Theories of Culture', *Annual Review of Anthropology*, Vol. 3, 1974, pp. 73-97.

72. R. K. Chatterjee, *Mass Communication* (National Book Trust, India) New Delhi, 1973, ' Introduction', p. 1.

73. *Ibid.*, p. 1.

74. Max Horkheimer and Thedor Adorno, *op. cit.*

75. Cited in R. K. Chatterjee, *op. cit.*, p. 91.

76. Cited in J. C. Mathur, *New Lamps for Aladdin*, (Mass Media in Developing Societies), Orient Longmans, New Delhi, 1965.

77. See extracts from a report originally prepared for the Commonwealth Broadcasting Conference held in Australia (Sydney) in 1956 and subsequently brought uptodate after the UNESCO project of Radio Form Forums, in J. C. Mathur, *op, cit.*, p. 104.

78. *Ibid.*, p. 104.

79. *Ibid.*, p. 111.

80. R. K. Chatterjee, *op. cit.*, p. 65.

81. *Ibid.*, pp. 66, 80.
82. Subir Ghosh, *Mass Communication Today : In the Indian Context*, Profile Publishers, Kolkata.
83. Broadcast talk by N.K. Rustomji on the occasion of Independence May 1960, in Elwin Papers, I found a separate file on these broadcasts, p. 1.
84. *Ibid.*, p. 4.
85. File No. 52, p. 1.
86. Elwin Papers, File No. ATA/G/14, listed as File No. 54, p. 20.
87. *Ibid.*
88. *Ibid.*, p. 22.
89. R.K. Chatterjee, *op, cit.*, p. 8.
90. See P.N. Malhan, *Communication Media : Yesterday, Today and Tomorrow* (Publication Division, Ministry of Information and Broadcasting, Government of India, New Delhi), 1985, p. 139; R.K. Chatterjee, *op. cit.*, p. 97.
91. P.N. Malhan, *op. cit.*, p. 139.
92. *Ibid.*, p. 140.
93. *Ibid.*, p. 140.
94. Ronald Inden, Transnational class, erotic Arcadia and Commercial Utopia in Hindi Films' in *Christiane* Brosius and Melissa Butcher, eds, *Image Journeys* : Audio-visual Media and cultural change in India, Sage Publication, New Delhi, Thousand Oaks, London, 1999, p. 48.
95. *Ibid.*, p. 50.
96. *Ibid.*, p. 47.
97. Quoted in P. N. Malhan, *op, cit*, p. 142.
98. Quoted by Britta Ohm 'Doordarshan : Representing the Nation's State' in Christiane Brosius and Melissa Butched, ed., *op. cit.*, p. 82.
99. Arvind Singhal and Everett. M. Rogers, *India's Information Revolution*. (Sage, New Delhi, 1989), p. 85.
100. This section is an extension of the paper presented at Eighteenth session of the North-East India History Association held in 1997 in Tripura University, Agartala and was published in the *Proceedings of North-East India History Association*,

Agartala, 1997, titled "Nationalist Hegemony and Popular Culture in Arunachal Pradesh : A Case Study of responses to Video-Cinema in Doimukh Circle of Papum-Pare District", pp. 291-302. This was based on the fieldwork conducted in Doimukh circle. But subsequently as part of the project sponsored by ICHR, New Delhi, I extended the field work in the Siang valley and therefore this section is a revised version based on this field work.

101. Quoted in Sumita Chakravarty, *Identity and Authenticity : Nationhood and the Popular Indian Cinema*, 1947-62, Ph.D. Thesis, University of Illinois, Nehru Memorial Centre for Contemporary Studies, Teen Murti House, New Delhi, p. 50.

102. *Ibid.*

103. Richard Dyer, 'Entertainment and Utopia' in Simon During, ed., *The Cultural Studies Reader*, Routledge, London, 1993, p. 273.

104. *Ibid.*, p. 287.

105. Louis Althusser, 'Ideology and Ideological State Apparatus' *Lenin and Philosophy*, trans. Ben Brewster (New Left Books, 1971), p. 162.

106. *Ibid.*, p. 163.

107. I have derived this idea from Bertold Brecht, *Brecht on Theatre*, Hill and Wang, 1964.

108. Benedict Anderson, *Imagined Communities*, Reflections on the origin and spread of Nationalism, Verso London, 1983, p. 15.

109. Sumita Chakravarty, *op. cit.*, p. 192.

110. Michel Foucault, *Power/Knowledge : Selected Interviews and Other Writings* : 1972-73, ed., Colin Gordon, *et al.*, New York, 1980, p. 73.

111. Sumita Chakravarty, *op.cit.*, p. 74.

112. Pierre Bourdieu, 'The aristocracy of Culture', *Media, Culture, Society*, Vol. 2, No. 3, 1980, p. 225.

113. Raymond Williams, *Keywords*, London, reprinted ed., 1984, pp. 313-15.

114. *Ibid.*, p. 313.

115. *Ibid.*

116. *Ibid.*

117. *Ibid.*, pp. 314 - 15.

118. The concept of 'civilising discourse' taken from Norbert Elias, *The Civilising Process*, Vol. 1 (The History of Manners), tr. E. Jephcott, New York, Pantheon, 1978.

119. Pierre Bourdieu, *Outline of a Theory of Practice*, tr. R. Nice, Cambridge, 1977, pp. 94-95.

120. I have borrowed the concept of 'common-sense' from Antonio Gramsci, *Selections From Prison Note Books, op. cit.*, pp. 322-323; Arun Kumar Patnaik, 'Gramsci's concept of Common Sense', *Economic and Political Weekly*, January, 30, 1988, pp. PE-2 to PE-10.

121. N. Poulantzas, *State, Power, Socialism*, New Left Books, 1987, p. 58.

122. Roland Barthes, *The Pleasure of Text*, Cape, 1978, p. 28.

123. V. N. Volosinov, *Marxism and the Philosophy of Language*, Academic Press, 1973.

Chapter - 3
Educated Class, Identity Crisis and Intellectuals

I

The emergence of the new educated social group was faster as a result of the faster developmental activities in the post Indo-China war of 1962. The Literacy percentage for 1961 and 1971 as per Census[1] is given below :

Arunachal Pradesh/District	*Total Rural Urban*	*1971*	*1961*
Arunachal Pradesh	Total	11.29	7.13
Kameng		9.61	8.74
Subansiri		6.89	4.24
Siang		12.97	7.24
Lohit		17.39	13.07
Tirap		11.22	5.16

Scheduled Tribes

Arunachal Pradesh/District	*Total*	*1971*	*1961*
Arunachal Pradesh	Total	5.20	2.51
Kameng		3.26	1.98
Subansiri		3.16	0.86

Siang	7.71	3.69
Lohit	7.38	5.40
Tirap	4.76	1.79

Source : Census of India 1971, Series I p. xiv

The above table clearly brings out the growth of literacy in the area of our study, that is the Siang district (at that time Siang district had not yet been divided into more districts). From 1961 to 1971 the percentage of literacy in this district rose from 7.24 to 12.97 while the percentage of literacy in case of Scheduled Tribe population in this district from 1961 to 1971 was 3.69 to 7.71. The total percentage of literacy including the Scheduled Tribe population in 1981 and 1991 was (Arunachal Pradesh) : 25.55 and 41.59 respectively.[2] The Adis inhabit in West Siang, East Siang districts and also a percentage of Adi population (Padam sub-tribe) inhabits Debang Valley. The percentage of literacy for 1991 in the West Siang, East Siang and Dibang valley is : 45.64, 44.30 and 44.88 respectively. Therefore, we find that there has been a progressive growth of the literacy percentage of Adis from 1961 to 1991.

The educated class has played a significant role in bringing about changes in Arunachal Pradesh. Investigating this process of change in agriculture in the three districts of Arunachal Pradesh–West Siang, Lower Subansiri and Papumpare and applying the sophisticated tools of institutional economics, N.C. Roy and P.K. Kuri in their project report, *A Study of Land Reform in Arunachal Pradesh (1997)* argue that it was 'the centrality of education, which was the major actor in bringing about a series of changes in agriculture :

> In post-independence period, Arunachal Pradesh witnessed many institutional changes occurring in her agriculture. The communal ownership of land was replaced by individual ownership...In the establishment of individual property rights in land education has played the most instrumental role...The centrality of education in the whole process of changes in agrarian institutions is derived from its role in the extension of transaction space beyond the communal boundaries. All other agents–infrastructural facilities, such as roads, transport

> and communications, hospital and above all Government's administrative services which created the intertribal space seem to have worked through the medium of human capital, mainly education. In post-independent period being educated meant coming out of the communal boundaries... education... has been the main force behind all inequalities and all differentiations.[3]

Here, in fact, culture seems to have played the role of basis instead of being relegated to the status of 'superstructure'. In fact the analogy of 'basis' and 'superstructure', former representing the economic and the later 'culture' is not very useful in understanding the changes occurring in Arunachal Pradesh. In this context the reciprocal interaction of basis and superstructure has to be emphasised.[4] "Without production no history" says R.S. Sharma,[5] but "without culture no production," adds E.P. Thompson. "Class, in the Marxist tradition, continues E.P. Thompson" is (or ought to be) a historical category; describing *people in relationship over time*, and the ways in which they become conscious of their relationships, separate, unite, enter into struggle, form institutions and transmit values in class ways."[6] In this respect, the French thinker, Pierre Bourdieu's ideas on the 'culture of living' (life-style) as an area of struggle between social groups and classes, are very useful in understanding the changing society of Arunachal Pradesh. For Bourdieu, the consumption of culture is "predisposed, consciously and deliberately or not, to fulfil a social function of legitimating social differences."[7] Culture is used by the dominant class, according to Bourdieu, to ensure its reproduction as the dominant class. Bourdieu interrogates "the processes by which the making of cultural distinctions secures and legitimates forms of power and domination which are ultimately rooted in economic inequality."[8] He argues that "although class rule is ultimately economic, the form which it takes is cultural; and that cultural distinction, the making, marking and maintaining of cultural difference, is the key to understanding this."[9] Thus the source of difference "is symbolically shifted from the economic field to the field of culture, making power appear to be the result of cultural distinciton."[10]

II

Migration, Growth of Population and Identity Crisis

Urbanisation and Migration are important indicators of economic development and social change. In the post-independent NEFA there had been migration (internal) of the population from one rural area to another and from rural to urban areas.[11] According to 1971 census, the percentage of internal migrant population was 31-83% of the total population of the state and it increased to 35.58 of the total population of the state of 1981.[12]

Table - 1

Total and Male Migrants Classified By Distance Covered in the Districts of Arunachal Pradesh, 1981

(In percentage)

Sl. No.	*District*	*Distance Covered*					
		Intra-district	*Rank-ing*	*Inter-district*	*Rank-ing*	*Inter-state*	*Rank-ing*
1	2	3	4	5	6	7	8
1.	West Kameng	47.79 (40.01)	5 (5)	4.23 (4.35)	9 (9)	47.98 (55.64)	4 (3)
2.	East Kameng	75.68 (56.78)	2 (2)	7.38 (8.58)	3 (3)	16.94 (34.64)	8 (8)
3.	Lower Subansiri	62.59 (47.54)	4 (4)	4.96 (5.51)	7 (6)	32.45 (46.95)	6 (6)
4.	Upper Subansiri	80.03 (63.32)	1 (1)	6.97 (8.04)	4 (4)	13.00 (28.64)	9 (9)
5.	West Siang	67.23 (52.18)	3 (3)	5.90 (6.36)	5 (5)	26.87 (41.46)	7 (7)
6.	East Siang	42.23 (35.93)	7 (7)	11.14 (10.10)	2 (2)	46.23 (53.97)	5 (5)
7.	Diband Valley	33.64 (22.76)	8 (9)	13.36 (12.15)	1 (1)	53.00 (65.09)	2 (2)

(Contd. . .)

(Contd. .

1	2	3	4	5	6	7	8
8.	Lohit	33.18 (25 22)	9 (8)	4.65 (4.47)	8 (8)	62.17 (70.31)	1 (1)
9.	Tirap	46.14 (39.95)	6 (6)	5.49 (5.52)	6 (7)	48.37 (54.83)	3 (4)

Figures in the bracket indicate the percentage distribution of male migrants.

Source : Taken from A. Mitra, Internal Migration and Economic development in the Hills. Omson Publications, New Delhi, 1997, p. 57.

Table - 2

Migrants from Major States of India to Arunachal Pradesh 1986

S. No.	*State*	*Total*
1.	Assam	51,526
2.	Bihar	11,436
3.	Uttar Pradesh	7,250
4.	West Bengal	4,060
5.	Meghalaya	2,287
6.	Kerala	2,237
7.	Other States	10,478
	Total	89,274

Source : Computed from Census of India, 1991, Migration Tables, Arunachal Pradesh, Part V A & B, Series-25.

Table -3

The Total Migrants Classified by Direction of Movement in Case of Arunachal Pradesh, 1981

(in Percentage)

S. No.	*Direction of movement*	*Total*
1.	Rural to Rural	79.40
2.	Rural to urban	9.63
3.	Urban to Rural	7.51
4.	Urban to Urban	3.46

Source : Computed taken from Census of India, 1981 Migration Tables of Arunchal Pradesh, Part V A & B, Series - 25.

The growth of urban settlements in Arunachal Pradesh seems to be direct outcome of political and administrative development of the state."[13] In the 1961 census, none of the places in Arunachal Pradesh satisfied the criteria of being declared as census town and hence the entire state was declared as rural.[14] However, some of the districts and sub-divisional headquarters of the state were found to be possessing distinct urban characteristics in 1971.[15] Accordingly Bombdila, Pasighat, Tezu and Along were treated as census towns during the 1971 census.[16] As per 1991 census the total urban population of Arunachal Pradesh was 104,806, that is, it formed 12.21% of the total population of the state.[17] In 1981 it formed 6.56% while in 1991 it rose to 12.21%. The number of towns as per 1991 census was 10.[18] The Decennial growth rate of urban population from 1981-1991 was 152.98. In the three districts where Adi population is predominant the following table indicates the percentage of population :

Table - 4

S. No.	*State/District*	*1981*	*1991*
1.	Arunachal Pradesh	6.52	12.21
2.	West Siang	11.82	12.36
3.	East Siang	11.98	14.53
4.	Dibang Valley	—	16.94

Source : Census of India 1991, Series - 1, Paper - 2 of 1991, p. 15.

Growth of Population

One of the significant aspects of the growth of population of Arunachal Pradesh is that the percentage of population of outsiders/outside migrants/non-tribal population has been progressively been increasing after Indo-China war of 1962 as a result of faster growth of developmental activities. The following tables based on 1991 census indicates this process.

Table - 5
Percentage Decadal Variation of Population, 1961 to 1991

	1961-71	*1971-81*	*1981-1991*
Total	+ 38.91	+ 35.15	+ 36.83
Rural	+ 33.77	+ 31.14	+ 27.70
Urban	—	+ 139.63	+ 167.04

Source : Census 1991, *op. cit.*, p. 98.

Percent Distribution of India's Total, Schedule Caste, Schedule Tribe and None Schedule Caste/Schedule Tribe Population - (I am taking only the case of Arunachal Pradesh):

Table - 6

	1981	*1991*
1. Schedule Caste	0.46	0.47
2. Schedule Tribe	69.82	63.66
3. Non S.C./S.T.	29.72	35.87

Source : Computed from Census, 1991, *op. cit.*, p. 40.

Decadal Growth rate of Total Scheduled caste, scheduled tribe and Non-Scheduled Caste/Scheduled Tribe Population in Case of Arunachal Pradesh for the period 1981 - 1991 was :

Table - 7

Total Population	*Scheduled Caste*	*Scheduled Tribe*	*Non-SC/ST*
36.83	38.81	24.75	65.19

Source : Computed from Census - 1991, *op. cit.*, p. 44.

Therefore, we find that the percentage of non-tribal population in comparison to the Tribal population from 1981 to 1991 had grown which is a quite significant phenomenon from the perspective of our study.

Identity Crisis

The migration, internal as well as from outside the state, the growing urbanisation, institutional changes in agriculture, various changes in the traditional occupations have threatened the traditional way of living, especially of the educated class and therefore created an identity crisis in the society. However, it were the intellectuals who were able to articulate this identity crisis and gave it a coherent form. But the nomenclature 'Intellectuals' has to be clarified. Who constitutes the 'intellectual' in the context of Arunachal Pradesh? Can the entire educated class be termed as intellectual? A brief discussion on these aspects is desired.

Intellectuals/Intelligentsia Educated Middle Class

The nomenclature 'intellectual' has to be distinguished from 'intelligentsia'. Writing about the colonial intelligentsia in the context of their role in India from mid-nineteenth century onwards Professor Sabyasachi Bhattacharya points out : "all intellectuals are members of the intelligentsia or almost all are - but not every member of the intelligentsia is an intellectual."[19] Edward Shill's definition of intellectuals includes "civil service, journalism, law, teaching (particularly college and University, but also secondary school teaching), and medicine."[20] According to Shill these professions "require either intellectual certification or Intellectual skill."[21] But Profession Sabyasachi Bhattacharya argues "not all these professions allow its members to function in society as intellectuals."[22] Here, we recall Antonio Gramsci's paradox that "in a sense all men are intellectuals, but not all perform the function of intellectuals."[23] Marx, in German Ideology, called intellectual's "active, conceptive ideologists."[24] Therefore, in this sense, they are the transmitters of ideology. Writing about the intellectuals and their role in cultural and ideological struggle against colonialism in India, Professor K. N. Panikkar writes :

> Basically they were non-conformists, critical of existing social conditions and performing the social function of generation or adoption and propagation of ideas with a view to ushering in socio-political progress and advancement.[25]

We would be using he concept of intellectuals in this broader perspective (in the sense Prof. K. N. Panikkar has used). Thus writers, literary writers as well, public men, journalists and thinkers etc., would be put in this category of 'intellectuals' in our study.[26]

It were the intellectuals in NEFA [Arunachal Pradesh] who gave a coherent form to the identity crisis and led the movement for cultural identity. There have been large number of intellectuals whom I have interviewed (among the Adis, the subject of this study) but the most prominent among them have been : Oshong Ering, Talom Rukbo, Lummar Dai, Tumpak Ete., Dagmo Jini, Tagang Taki and Jarjum Ete.

The movement for cultural identity has been perceived and expressed in various ways by these intellectuals. One of the aspects of this movement is the response to the spread of Christianity, which would be discussed in the next chapter. It also expressed in the formation of Cultural and Literary societies, recording of myths, legends or in other words, recovery of their past/traditions/history (these categories are used interchangeably). The movement for forging religious identity based on the indigeneous traditions also forms one of the important aspects of the movement for cultural identity. The reformation of certain selective cultural practices has been an important agenda of this movement and related to it is the question of women's status. But it is the women intellectuals themselves who have taken this question more effectively. All these issues would be taken up in the subsequent chapters.

REFERENCES

1. Census of India, 1971, Series - 1.
2. Census of India, 1991, Series 1, Paper 2 of 1991, p. 53.
3. N. C. Roy and P. K. Kuri, *A Study of Land Reform in Arunachal Pradesh*, Report of The Project Sponsored by ICSSR, New Delhi, 1997, pp. 160-61
4. E. P. Thompson, 'Folklore, Anthropology and Social History, in *The Indian Historical Review*, January 1977, Volume, III Number, 2, p. 258.
5. Cited in E. P. Thompson, *ibid.*, p. 264.
6. *Ibid.*, **p. 264.**

7. Pierre Bourdieu, *Distinction*, Harvard University Press, Cambridge, 1984, p. 5.
8. John Storey, *Cultural Studies and the Study of Popular Culture : Theories and Methods* Edinburg University Press, Edinburgh, 1996, p. 116.
9. *Ibid.*
10. *Ibid.*
11. See A. Mitra, *Internal Migration & Economic Development in the Hills*, Omson Publications, New Delhi, 1997, pp. 50-73.
12. Cited in *Ibid.*, p. 50.
13. A. Mitra, op. cit., p. 105
14. *Ibid.*
15. *Ibid.*
16. *Ibid.*
17. Census of India, 1991, Series - 1.
18. *Ibid.*
19. Sabyasachi Bhattacharya, "Notes on the role of the Intelligentsia in colonial society : India from mid nineteenth century", *Studies in History*, Vol. I, Number 1, January-June 1979, p. 98.
20. Quoted in Sabyasachi Bhattacharya, *op. cit.*, p. 98.
21. *Ibid.*, p. 98.
22. *Ibid.*
23. Antonio Gramsci, *Selections from the Prison Notebooks, op. cit.*, p. 9; also see Andre Beteille, *Ideologies and Intellectuals*, New Delhi, 1980, pp. 44-45.
24. Kari Marx, *German Ideology*, edition of 1965, London, p. 61.
25. K. N. Panikkar, "The Intellectual History of Colonial India : Some Historiographical and Conceptual Questions" in Sabyasachi Bhattacharya and Romila Thapar, eds. *Situating Indian History*, Delhi, 1986, p. 412.
26. Prof. Bipan Chandra has used this term in this sense in his work on the ideology of Nationalism in nineteenth century India. See *The Rise and Growth of Economic Nationalism in India*, New Delhi, 1969, p. 752.

Chapter - 4
Responses to Christianity

The proselytisation to Christianity and the presence of outside religions created a sense of 'other' among the people of Arunachal Pradesh, especially the Adis. Therefore, their response to outside religions represents an aspect of their cultural identity. It is therefore, worthwhile to narrate in brief the history of Christianity in Arunachal Pradesh, especially among the Adis.

I

A BRIEF OUTLINE OF THE HISTORY OF CHRISTIANITY IN ARUNACHAL PRADESH

The history of conversion of the tribes of Arunachal can be traced back to nineteenth century when the American Baptist Missionaries opened Sadiya as a Mission Station in 1836.[1] But it is only in the last decade of the nineteenth century that the local tribes started accepting the Christian faith.[2] According to John Selander's Report of 1937 the Sadiya Mission Station school had about fifty 'Abor' (Adi) boys in the Boarding on Easterday and he himself had baptised three Adi (Abor) boys.[3] The first convert to Christianity was a Padam-Abor named Dugyon.[4] He had studied in Jorhat and had helped the Missionaries in translation work. Through his help sixty-four pages Abor-Song book was written besides The Gospels of Mark, Luke and John and Acts.[5]

Agents of Conversion

According to the Christian sources the agents of conversion were the tribal boys educated in the Sadiya Mission school.[6] Having finished their education they were sent back to their villages to spread the 'message of Christ.'[7] It is evident from a statement made by Alexander Mar Thoma, Metropolitan, Mar Thoma Church, Tiruvala on February 19, 1979 :

> It is obligatory on the part of Christians to communicate the 'revealed truth' to others. For them profession and practice of religion involves sharing and communication of their spiritual experience.[8]

M.A.Z. Rolston, the General Secretary of the National Council of Christians of India, wrote in 1979 :

> What is remarkable about this young church is that it has grown mainly through the endeavours of the few young tribals who came into contact with Christians mainly in educational institutions outside Arunachal Pradesh. They accepted Christ and when they went back to their own people they shared their faith with them.[9]

He further states :

> Many opponents of the church in Arunachal Pradesh insinuate that the growth of the church in Arunachal is spreading influence of foreigners in that state. But there are no foreign missionaries involved there, for the only missionaries active in Arunachal are the young educated tribals who have accepted Christ and who propagate their faith among their friends, relatives and neighbours.[10]

II

RESPONSES TO CHRISTIANITY

(A) Official Response

The official attitude to conversion was marked by hostility. It can be comprehended in the light of the discourse provided by the policy-makers during 1950's.[11] the tenor of this discourse as discussed in the second chapter of this book was

" to develop the tribes along the lines of their own tradition and genius."[12] The critique of Christian missionaries formed an important aspect of this discourse since the former was perceived to be antithetical to tribal cultural practices. Thus Elwin wrote :

> In many places the effect of their teaching has been to break-up families and divide villages. One may see a village, which at one time worked and lived as a single unit, now split into a Christian and a non-Christian hamlet. In one tribal village no fewer than five different missions were carrying on propaganda, opening separate schools and teaching different forms of Christianity. The effect on the simple tribal mind can easily be imagined. The attitude of some missionaries has been completely destructive of the tribal culture.
>
> To them everything which is not Christian is 'heathen' and some of the finest aspects of tribal life have been abandoned. Dance and songs, even the weaving of lovely textiles and the traditional tribal institutions have perished before their intolerance. The tribals have been taught to despise their past and as a result a strong inferiority complex has been created.[13]

G.A. Smali, a retired I.C.S. had expressed similar views as early as 1946 :

> The opening of the schools in the Hills has also been opposed by the non-Christians, because there are no non-Christian teachers, and the entry of Christianity into a village means end of all tribal customs. Tribal dances are forbidden, and the drinking of the home-made rice beer means excommunication.[14]

Even Nehru, whose secular credentials were beyond doubt, had developed attitude marked by ambivalence towards some of the foreign missionaries activities in the North-East India. He lauded them for their commitment to tribal welfare in the field of education and health.[15] But at the same time he criticised them for encouraging "narrow-mindedness, distinct from the true Christian spirit and values" among the converts.[16] He was not opposed to evangelical work *per se* but to their political campaign.[17]

Nehru's attitude to Christian missionaries operating in the North-Eastern parts of India, was governed to some extent by coming to grip with the question of movement for Naga nationalism. Some foreign missionaries were perceived to be inculcating "certain anti-Indian feelings."[18] In the Naga Hills, says Professor S. Gopal, "some of the British Missionaries were former officials who had not yet come to terms with the political changes in India."[19] In a note on a tour of the North-Eastern Frontier Areas, Nehru wrote :

> Their chief experience of outsiders was that of British officers and Christian missionaries, who generally tried to make them anti-Indian. As Indian Independence gradually approached and it became obvious that British rule was coming to an end in India, some of these British officers and Christian missionaries induced them to think in terms of independence. This had some effect on some sections of the Nagas.[20]

And since 1947, "a heavy influx into India of missionaries from the United States" had taken place. According to Prof. Gopal, "their very presence" implied political impact in Nehru's perception. As Nehru wrote to Amrit Kaur, "Americanism is not only a particular way of life but a particular way of thinking in politics. In the present context of the world this becomes politics directly."[21] It seems Nehru's perceptions were coloured by cold-war between two super powers and the type of politics pursued by the American Government in the third world countries. Emerging directly out of the anti-imperialist struggle and intending to develop the Indian society along the socialist path it was natural on his part to suspect any cultural or religious organisation coming from an aggressive imperialist nation.

According to Elwin, "the singularly narrow and intolerant Christianity (a parody of liberal and urbane faith of the modern world)" had the "psychological effect of making the Christian Nagas feel superior to and apart from their 'heathen' brethren in Hindu India." Elwin perceived close relationship between missionary activities and their philanthropic work :

> I do not think it is possible for any good missionary really to confine himself to merely educational and medical work. If he

is sincere he is bound to try to convert the people among whom he works.[22]

One of the political officer, Tezu, Lt. Col. G. S. Puri in his Tour Diary reported that amongst the younger generation of Christians in The Padam and Idus area "consider themselves superior to their own brethren" and "are neither prepared to work in the fields nor and they prepared to work earnestly when offered Government Job." Such people, according to him "are living in a world of their own creation and look down with suspicion any activities of the Administration and indulge in spreading wrong propaganda against the Government."[23]

Thus the official hostility to Christianity was marked by complexity.

(B) Indigeneous Responses

The indigeneous leaders were opposed to the missionaries' activities since they perceived a threat to the survival of their traditional culture. These leaders were either pursuing their education outside NEFA or they after having completed their education were either employed in Government offices or were involved in public activities. These leaders expressed their views in a petition dated 22nd April, 1971 from MIRMIR village (adjoining Pasighat town) submitted to the then Prime Minister of India, Smt. Indira Gandhi.[24] This petition was signed by (*a*) Secretary, Bogum Bokang Kebang, Siang District; (*b*) President Milum Kebang, Pasighat; and (*c*) Secretary, Monga Padam Bango, Left Bank, Mebo. This petition was submitted as a reaction to the report by Adi converts to Christianity submitted to the Prime Minister and signed by : "Sarbashree Onong Perme, Oling Ratan, Tojing Pertin, Skodong Pertin and Kaku Pertin from Kiyit, Ngopok Village and Sarbashree Anggong Ratan, Tasi Dupak, Kepiam Yirang etc., from Dapi village during January 1971."[25] The petition submitted by the indigeneous leaders alleged that the converts' report distorted the entire issue. Since this petition is a long document and provides an insight into the indigeneous leaders' perception of the 'other', it needs a detailed elaboration.

The document constructs the concept of 'other' first of all by tracing the history of Christianity in the Siang district. Here Christianity and colonialism are conceptualised as synonymous. It states that the imperialists attempted to rule the Adis by force, conversion, opium and finally through mission schools. But all these attempts failed to subjugate them:

> During the British Rule there were attempts to convert us into Christianity but they were not successful in doing so as we vehemently opposed it. The Britishers while trying to rule us, a freedom loving people by force suffered a lot of setbacks in Siang district. Lot of army personnel got killed. Besides this a Reverend was also a victim in late 1911-12. Being unable to place us under their control the Britisher then tried to convert us into Christianity in order to befriend us and gradually bring us under their control. When this also failed, the Britishers then introduced opium in NEFA with the intention to liquidate us. During the 2nd World War those who went as porters in the North Burma war Theatre they were given opium as ration and also as payment for portering loads. While receiving all these set backs the British rulers then succeeded in establishing a school at Sadiya, then southern most administrative centre of NEFA. The try for converting us into Christianity was then entrusted on one Rev. Sanderson operating from Sadiya and Rev. Larsen operating from Dibrugarh. A handful of Adi Padam and Gallongs were then baptised.[26]

The petitioners of this document made a distinction between the earlier (earlier generation) converts and those who embraced Christianity in the post-independence period, that is the younger generation of converts. The earlier converts, according to the leaders of this petition, not only did not proselytise the people but also participated in all the social and cultural fastivities.[27] They never indulged into flaunting the new religious faith. Setting examples of social service, restraint and discipline the early converts were being regarded with esteem by the indigeneous leaders and they also in turn, started venerating Jesus Christ.[28] The later converts, on the other hand, were alleged to be the harbingers of disharmony. These Adi Christian converts not only started flaunting their new religious faith but also ridiculing the indigeneous faith and practices. Their attitude smacked of arrogance and superiority complex *vis-à-vis* the non-converts.[29]

The petitioners alleged that the strategy adopted by the converts to Christianity among the Adis to defame and "crush down the Adi belief" are manifold. Some of these are :

(i) The present Adi Christian converts receiving free Christian religious literatures and money from Lakhimpur, Tezpur, Gauhati, Dibrugarh, Shillong and Nowgang in the State of Assam are influencing the Adi simple villagers and mostly childrens in large number and are converting them into Christians. First, they start with singing of hymns and carols and then free illustrated leaflets on Christianity together with a Bible is distributed. In prayer meeting the leaders do not forget to explain more elaborately that the Gate to Heaven is only open to Christians and no one else will be allowed to enter Heaven. Of late the Adi Christian converts have started to advertise that within 5 (five) years entire NEFA will become a home of Christian and in 15 (fifteen) years entire India will embracing Christianity. To a literate this propaganda does not mean anything but for an illiterate and child it is quite opposite.

(ii) To impress upon the illiterate mass the present Adi converts openly denounce the Kebangs held in villages. The Kebang is one of our most important meeting where we in generally decide in a collective way all our issues. The practice is a very age-old custom of ours. Only to show that they belong to a separate entity the Adi Christian converts had stopped participating in all social, communal works. Especially on Sundays no Adi Christian shall budge an inch to do any good social or communal work.

(iii) To further put up a show of their separate entity they have stopped joining in the local Adi communal feasts and communal gatherings. They, the Adi Christian

converts have started changing their eating and drinking habits. They have stopped eating flesh of trapped or sacrificed animals stating that it is against Christianity, few have started giving up drinking of 'APONG' the traditional rice bear. It is a tradition for an Adi to offer APONG to maternal uncle, in-laws and near relatives and friends during auspicious days, festivals, communal feasts and gatherings. This have given rise to discontentment amongst customary relationships between a non-Christian Adi relative with a Christian relative leaving aside others.

(iv) Adi Christians have started evading to visit ailing non- Christian relative even if he or she be his own brother or sister.

(v) While giving up all Adi age-old culture, custom and religion the Adi Christian converts have started criticising the non-Christian Adi people and displaying hatred.

(vi) Contradicting all Kebang works, the Adi Christians do not at all participate in any good Kebang works.[30]

All this according to the petitioners, have created disharmony and discord in the egalitarian Adi society. The leaders assert that they have strong belief in religious universalism and unity of mankind but the preaching by the "so-called Adi Christian converts of Siang" are in contradiction to these principles. The petitioners allege that the converts are "preaching in the following lines" :

(1) Hindu, Muslim, Sikh, Buddhists and other religions are of small category having less followers and do not worship the right God.

(2) In the world the person following Christianity become richer people, they are now landing on the moon, they can fight wars and of all-important point is that Christians are in large number than any other religious group in the world.

(3) The people of Nagaland being Christians can fight the Indian Government. MIJO and Khasis similarly being Christian can do anything against Indian Government.

(4) While preaching amongst young boys and girls the SIANG Adi Christians state that there is no need of schools, if they become Christians the American Government shall help them in all ways and means.

(5) Christianity is recognised by the United nations while Hindu religion is practised in India only and Hindu religion is not practised anywhere else.[31]

Therefore, the petitioners requested "the Government to arrest all person indulging in preaching religions other than local indigeneous tribal religious belief for helping uplift and maintain our own traditional religion and culture especially within NEFA."[32]

The document clearly states :

> We do not want Adis to be converted in any other religion whatsoever it may be we want to maintain our own religion and culture. "It is the Christians especially, who do not what us to maintain our religion and customs and they are placing obstacles even in the Adi cultural sphere." The Government is requested to take strong steps against such persons and others likewise steps against those who advocate for spreading and practicing Christianity amongst he Adi NEFA tribals. We do not want our sons and daughters to be converted into Christianity and no one should entice us by giving monetary help in name of aid with the view of converting us into Christianity. One ordinary man or be he a minister also he should respect and abide by our old customary Kebang systems. It will be wrong within NEFA to form a separate Christian society to bring a division amongst us. In our Adi area we will not allow construction of churches and we shall destroy same in case it is erected. We do not want a public display of Christianity, especially in Adi area. We have nothing to state about other areas. Does secularism mean freedom of the religion to dominate and destroy another religion because the former is richer and has large number of followers?[33]

Lastly the leaders pleaded in their petition to the Prime Minister of India "to help" them "from not getting disintegrated and remain one group as Adis and looking forward for all of" her "cooperation and help in enabling" them to "maintain" their "own religious belief and culture instead of going astray."[34]

III

STATE AND CIVIL SOCIETY

The official discourse and the indigeneous discourse on christianity seems to be synchronising. In other words, the State and Civil Society has been jointly working in NEFA to check the growth of Christianity. Without going in to the theoretical debate on the concept of civil society, I am using the concept in a very simple way, rather in too simplicit terms to denote various forums that mediate between the society and the state. I would be discussing some of the important forums created by the educated class in the later chapter but the document discussed in the preceding section was authored by the leaders of the indigeneous forums, that is Kebang, which is an age-old democratic institution of the Adis[35] and the other forum, that is Bogum Bokang was created under the guidance of the colonial officials[36] but later on appropriated by the indigeneous leaders of the society.

The Deputy Commissioner's order (Subansiri District) issued on December 11, 1975 would illustrate this :

> This is for general information of all that prior permission of the Government of Arunachal Pradesh is required before any place of worship such as churches, temple and mosque is made, failing which action will be taken to demolish them as unauthorised buildings.
>
> Permission is however, not required for building of houses of traditional worship, such as Donipolo Eugyang.
>
> Gaon Bora, etc., are required to give wide publicity to this order within their villages.[37]

The public spaces created by the educated classes in the form of Adi Cultural and Literacy Society got appropriated by the state in this regard as it is evident from their various correspondence with the officials. Thus, the Secretary, Adi cultural and Literacy society had been informing the officials about the conversions in the villages and also illegal construction of the temples, churches etc. Thus to quote from one of these letters :

1. There are 60 (sixty) Houses in Sille village out of which 9 (Nine) Houses have been converted to the Christianity.
2. Shri Tapon Ering and Shri Takeng Taying is the main leader of the party.
3. In every Sunday, there is Service at 9 A.M. in morning.
4. There is no permission to construct the church either from the government or village authority.
5. The villagers of Sille do not know any activities as the movements are very secret.[38]

In another letter, the Secretary, Adi cultural and Literary Society informed the Additional Deputy Commissioner, Pasighat about the resolution passed on 20th, and 21st, May 1977, at Ngorlung and Rayang villages respectively. The text of this Resolution is :

LUYIN AGOM (RESOLUTION)

Siloke Longeso Adi Cultural And Literary Society Troupe Em Dobo Sudula Luying Bosudung. Ngoluk Dolung Goraso Agike Adi Gide-Sipe Iyarla Duye Delokke Abit Dhorma Em Ngoluk Dolunguso Langa Mam Aye Delokke Dhormo Mondir At Imom Aye. [39]

(Today we sit together, we the members of the Adi cultural and Literary Society and decided that; we will continue do celebrate our festivals in the village and we will not allow other religions to enter into our area and will not allow to construct mandir (temple).

The Secretary, Adi Cultural and Literary Society further stated that "the villagers of both villages are strong and they requested for frequent vigilance of Adi leaders through cultural activities in those villages time to time."[40] He further informed the ADC (Additional District/Deputy Commissioner) that "in Rayang village there is only one person, Shri Gumin Gao by name, has converted to Christianity, that the villagers are not giving any facilities to him". He requested for "facilities to move the Adi cultural and Literacy Society troupe as and when required."[41] And the officials as revealed in documents had been readily complying with this request whenever it was made.

IV

VIOLENT RESPONSE

Resentment against proselytising activities took an aggressive form on the part of the indigeneous people in certain parts of NEFA. There is not much literature available on this aspect. Whatever archival sources I could trace was the mono-source, that is, the voice of the christian leaders from other parts of North-East India and India. Some of the voices I could recover were that of the indigeneous converts through interviews. But archival sources in this regard are non-existent. Therefore, both these accounts are being recounted here. The violence on converts' property started taking place from 1969 onwards.[42]

A meeting on May 6, 1975 took place at Doimukh for reconciliation.[43]

Simultaneously the various sects of christian missionary organisations in the North-East India expressed solidarity on the questions of "suffering" faced by the christian community of Arunachal Pradesh. Thus in the 39th. Meeting of the North-East India Christian Council held at Tura Baptist Church during May 6-9, 1976, the members appreciated the work of the Council in having organised a joint public meeting in Shillong by the Roman Catholic and the Protestant Churches "to express ecumenical unity on the Arunachal Christians sufferings" and "which later brought favourable situation to the Christians in Arunachal."[44]

V

MOVEMENT FOR DEMAND FOR PROTECTION OF INDIGENEOUS FAITH

There had been persistent demand from the people of Arunachal Pradesh since 1969 for "certain positive measures for preservation and promotion of their traditional culture and particularly their indigeneous faith."[45] This formed one of the four agendas of the fourth session of the NEFA Agency Council held at Shillong on the 12th and 13th. August 1971, under the chairmanship of the Governor of Assam.[46]

It was also taken up by the members of the Pradesh Council in its first session. The members expressed concern at the activities of certain outside agencies trying to influence the traditional culture of the local people.[47] According to the resolution adopted by the Pradesh Council on 5th October, 1972 :

> A person belonging to an indigeneous tribal community of Arunachal Pradesh who renounces the traditional belief or faith indigeneous to the community to which he or she belongs and takes to other belief and or faith should be deemed to have deserted the community/tribe and to have forfeited all facilities, benefits, advantages, considerations deriving from his or her being a member of that tribe/community.[48]

A similar resolution was passed by the Arunachal Pradesh Development-cum-cultural Convention held on May 21, 1976 at Pasighat. This convention was attended by over two thousand local leaders from all corners of Arunachal pradesh.[49] The resolution says :

> that any person belonging to any of the indigeneous tribes and communities of Arunachal Pradesh, who renounces the indigeneous belief and faith and takes to other belief and faith should be deemed to have deserted the community and should forfeit the facilities, benefits, and advantages and considerations deriving from his or her being a member of that tribe or community.[50]

The resolution urged upon the Government of Arunachal

Pradesh "to take immediate steps for implementation of the resolution."

In order to implement these resolutions the Chief Minister, Shri P. K. Thungon, therefore, introduced 'Arunachal Pradesh freedom of Indigeneous Faith 1978' Bill in the Arunachal Legislative Assembly for consideration of the House. It was taken up for discussion in the second session of the Legislative Assembly held from 17th May 1978 to 19th may, 1978. While introducing this bill the chief Minister commenting upon the earlier resolutions adopted by Agency council and Pradesh Council remarked :

> We have been considering various possibilities and ways of implementing this resolution which represents strong and spontaneous popular urge. The anxiety of the people for preservation of their traditional culture and faith is quite genuine. It is borne out of a lurking fear in their minds that if no timely effective action is taken, their age-old culture and faith might be swarmed or overwhelmed by different culture and faith, alien to the society. We have also reports to indicate that there are forces operating inside the territory and their aim appears to be to subvert the traditional culture and faith of our people through unfair and principled means. These activities have resulted in unavoidable and undesirable friction in our society, as result there have been social tensions striking the very order of our society. The Government, therefore, considers it necessary to come forward with this piece of legislation. The primary object of this legislation is to meet the urge of the people for preservation of their age-old culture and secondly to avoid disposition of social peace and order.[51]

After discussion the bill was passed by the Arunachal Legislative Aseembly.[52] It was sent to the President of India for his assent.

VI

CHRISTIANS' RESPONSE TO THE BILL

While the President's assent to that Bill was awaited, the incidents of "violence against Christians re-occurred."[53] Consequently the National Christian Council of India invited representatives of various churches to meet in Delhi on 18th December 1978.[54] In that meeting several Christian MPs. Were present. Prof. V. V. John, a member of the Minorities Commission also attended that meeting. It provided an opportunity to representatives of the Church in Arunachal Pradesh," to inform the participants of the meeting, about the story of their harassment and persecution."[55] Consequently the meeting passed several resolutions which included the following :

1. To request the Minorities commission to look into the long-standing sufferings of the Arunachal Pradesh Christians.
2. To request Christian M.Ps. to visit Arunachal Pradesh and to get first hand information of the situation.[56]
3. To inform churches throughout the country about the sufferings of Arunachal Pradesh Christians and to appeal to observe the first Sunday in February (February 4, 1979) as day of prayer for Arunachal Pradesh.[57]
4. To request the Catholic Bishops' Conference of India and the National Christian Council of India to arrange for a joint meeting to determine the joint steps to be taken to meet the situation.[58]
5. To determine what legal steps may be necessary in regard to the Arunachal Pradesh Freedom of Religion Act, to ensure protection and security to the life and property of Christians and for safeguarding their right to practice, preach and propagate the faith of their choice.
6. To raise Rs. 10,00,000 to help Arunachal Pradesh christians in distress and to meet the expenses for the legal measures to be adopted.[59]

In a Memorandum to the President of India, some people on behalf of people of Arunachal urged the President "not to assent his approval to this unconstitutional and inhuman bill adopted by some religious fanatic under the guidance of Mr.

Raja Lt. Governor and P.K. Thungon, Chief Minister."[60] Mr. K.A.A. Raja was termed as 'colonial autocrate despot" and demanded his resignation :

> The people of Arunachal Pradesh have come to realise that Shri K. A. A. Raja, the despot ruler of Arunachal Pradesh through his shadow-puppet Khandu Government is at the root of all the *present* evils and miseries of the people of Arunachal Pradesh. He is consistently and systematically destroying all aspirations, hopes, ambitions and scopes/avenues, which could lead the people of Arunachal Pradesh to their economic advancement, happiness and prosperity. He is achieving his selfish fulfilments and colonial intents with the help of his small band of incompetent, anti-people, opportunistic bureacration (sic) admirers/courtiers who have raised a stinking smoke-screen around him only to amuse that everything is well with him and thereby fulfil their own vested selfish interests.
>
> *Will the Government of India therefore appreciate and help the progressive healthy aspirations of the Arunachal people and immediately remove the autocrat despot RAJA as a first positive step in this direction and thereby save Arunachal Pradesh?* (Emphasis original).[61]

Mrs. Rano Shaiza a member of Parliament and belonging herself to Christian community met the Prime Minister and drew his attention to the Bill. She told the Prime Minister "That the Bill is unconstitutional and anti-Christian and is particularly aimed at legalising the persecution of Christians."[62] Seeking to forestall the President's assent to the Bill, she said that "mischievous Bill was inspired by some anti christian administrators."[63] She also said that during the recent years, the Administration of Arunachal Pradesh has been on record for persecuting the christians involving the burning down of churches, employing the anti-social elements to perpetuate harassment to people belonging to Christian faith and systematically transferring christian employees of the Government. Mrs. Shaiza questioned the Government "Will the President of India who is committed to defend the constitution give his assent to such an unconstitutional legislations?"[64] She added, "inspite of the persecutions and unjust treatments, we the Christians of the country have in the past borne them as expected of us in the true Christian spirit to ensure that our right to freedom of religion and that of our fellow-citizens in Arunachal Pradesh is in no way usurped."[65]

VII

PRO-BILL VIEWS

The intellectuals who advocated protection of the indigeneous faith and practices condemned the reactions of the Christian leaders attitude to the 'Protection of indigeneous faith Bill'. The Adi intellectuals of this group started mobilising public opinion, especially of the intellectuals of other tribes of Arunachal Pradesh, in favour of the Bill. Thus Talom Rukbo wrote to all the Secretaries, of Cultural societies of Arunachal Pradesh pleading to mobilise public opinion in favour of the Bill and condemn the statement of Shri Bakin Pertin, Member of Parliament from Arunachal Pradesh and representing 'the opinion of the Christian of Arunachal Pradesh.[66]

In a resolution adopted by The Adi Cultural and Literary Society, Pasighat and forwarded to the President of India, New Delhi on 26ht August, 1978, it was stated :

> The Adi Cultural and Literary Society, Pasighat strongly opposed the statement of Shri Bakin Pertin and Christian M.P.'s against the indigeneous faith and belief Bill 1978 passed in Arunachal Assembly.
>
> This Bill is mainly meant for safeguard of our own traditional customs and socio-economic affairs. So President of India is earnestly requested not to accept the statement of Shri Bakin Pertin and other M. Ps.[67]

The office-bearers of the Adi Cultural and Literary society also proposed to organise a meeting at Pasighat where the representatives of the other cultural organisations of Arunachal Pradesh were proposed to be invited and a thorough discussion was proposed to be held on this question. Therefore, the Secretary, Adi Cultural and Literary Society, Pasighat sought financial assistance from the Lt. Governor of Arunachal

Pradesh for organising this meeting.[68] The Secretary expressed his opinion in this letter "Protest of Shri Bakin Pertin on indigeneous belief and faith Bill passed in the last Assembly meeting is becoming headache of Arunachal. And Christian States are also endorsing the statement of Shri Bakin Pertin."[69]

The Secretary, Adi Cultural and Literary Society, Pasighat wrote to the Secretary, Social and Cultural Affairs, Along, Roying Ziro and Bomdila to "send a resolution to the President of India against the statement of Shri Baking Pertin" and to "accept the indigeneous faith and belief Bill 1978 passed in Arunachal Assembly."[70] He wrote "We should not give any indulgence to create Christian State in Arunachal Pradesh where as our own customs and social activities are very strong."[71]

A 'Protest day' was observed by 'Arunachal Pradesh Social Reforms Federation' which was formed during September 1978, on 17th September 1978.[72] It was observed in protest against the delay by the President of India in giving his assent to the Freedom of indigeneous Faith Bill, passed by the Assembly. A public meeting, held on the occasion, adopted a resolution urging the President to give his assent to the Bill early.[73] It passed two other resolutions : (*a*) one to set up a Donyi-Polo (Sun and Moon God of the tribals) mission to preserve and protect tribal faiths and culture and the other to start Donyi-Polo calendar, with September 16 as the first day of the year.[74] The 'PWD Minister, Mr. Gagong Apong, who addressed the meeting, criticised the opposition to the Bill in Meghalaya, Nagaland and Mizoram and said this was 'undemocratic' and a 'clear interference'."[75] he said the people and their leaders in Arunachal Pradesh were mature enough to know what was good for them.[76]

A general meeting was proposed to be held on 5th October 1978 at Along to resolve safeguarding of indigeneous traditional culture and heritage.[77]

The intellectuals like Talom Rukbo, while his on tour of Bharat Darshan, met in person the President of India and requested him to "offer a soft corner to the people and approve the bill accordingly by his excellency."[78]

Finally, The President, Mr. Sanjiva Reddy, gave his assent to the controversial 'Arunachal Pradesh Freedom of Religion Bill, 1978' on 25th October 1978. It was called *The Arunachal Pradesh Freedom of Religion Act*. 1978 (Act No. 4 of 1978).[79] The said Act provided *inter-alia* vide section 3 that "no person shall convert or attempt to convert, either directly or otherwise, any person from one religious faith to any other religious faith by the use of force or by inducement or by any fraudulent means nor shall any person abet any such converson."[80]

A circular issued by the Additional Deputy Commissioner, Pasighat on November 8, 1979 stated :

> In the said act and rules *inter-alia* it has been provided that intimation should be given within 7 (seven) days to the Deputy Commissioner of the District to which the person converted belongs, of the fact of such conversion in the Form prescribed by the Government (available in the office of the Deputy Commissioner of this District) by the person who converts any person from one religious faith to any other religious faith either by performing himself the ceremony necessary for such conversion as a religious priest or by taking part directly or indirectly in such ceremony. If any person fails without sufficient cause to comply with the provisions contained in Sec. 5 (1) of the said Act, shall be punished with imprisonment which may extend shall be punished with imprisonment which may extend to one year or with fine which may extend to one thousand rupees or with both.

If any person contravenes any of the provisions of the said Act and Rules, the same should be reported to this office immediately.[81]

VIII

GROWTH OF CHRISTIANITY DESPITE THE PASSAGE OF BILL

Inspite of the passage of protection of indigeneous faith Bill Christianity in Arunachal Pradesh has been spreading by leaps and bounds as stated by the various groups of Christians and Christian missionaries.

L. Pizo from Gauhati reported :

> Inspite of signing the Freedom of Religion Bill, 1978 in Arunachal Pradesh and general suppression of conversion in the area, it has been reported that nearly 200 souls have come to Christ and new churches set-up. A good number of young people are reported to have seen vision and are speaking in tongues. They have given up their regular studies and have given their lives to serve Christ and his church.[82]

A Catholic view states that "inspite of this Bill, christianity is growing by leaps and bounds."[83]

> Not inspite of, but rather because of the persecution, the Arunachal Church is vibrant. It is evangelical and growing fast. It is a people's church, not a clerically dominant one. Arunachal has its own catholic union, with active participation. Tribesmen, gaily attired in hornbill headgear and bearsks sealbards, trek over 100 miles to attend the meeting![84]

The missionaries have been refuting the allegation that they are opposed to the local cultures.[85] There has been now an emphasis on integration of 'Christian ethos' with the 'local customs'. Thus in his first Christmas message in Arunachal, the Bishop Rt. Rev. Joseph Mittathany, DD; the Bishop of Tezpur who had come to preside the Christmas celebration at Lekhi (in the Nishing area and which was the scene of anti-Christian violence during 1970's) in December 1979, emphasized three aspects : *(a)* Patriotism, *(b)* Preservation of every 'good local custom' and *(c)* thus to incarnate Christian life into their environment.[86]

The rapid growth of Christianity is illustrated from the following tables taken from the Census figures :

Census Year	*Total Population*	*Christians Population*	*% to Total Population*
1961	336,558	1438	
1971	467,511	3,684	0.79
1981	631,839	27,306	
1991	864,558	89,013	

The percentage increase in the population of the

Christians from 1981 to 1991 was 225.98 which was the largest in comparison to other communities' percentage of increase in population, therefore, naturally it had been alarming the indigeneous intellectuals of Arunachal Pradesh, especially the Adi intellectuals.

REFERENCES

1. N. P. Mason, *These Seventy Five Years,* cited in M. S. Sangma, 'Attempts to Christianize the people of Arunachal Pradesh by the American Baptist Missionaries (1836-1950), *Proceedings of North-East India History Association*, Pasighat. 1986 (seventh session), p. 263.
2. M.A.Z. Rolston, 'Persecution of Christians in Arunachal Pradesh; *National Council of Christian Review*, Vol. XCIX, No. I, January 1979, p. 73. (Now-on-wards mentioned as NCCR).
3. John Selander, *Report from Dibru-Sadiya Field,* 35th, Session of the American Baptist Conference, Sadiya, December 8-13, 1937, cited in M. S. Sangma, *op. cit.*, p. 269.
4. *Ibid.*
5. *Ibid.*
6. *NCCR*, Vol, XCIX, No. 4, April 1979, p. 222.
7. *Ibid.*
8. *Ibid.*
9. M.A.Z. Rolston, *op. cit.*, p. 73.
10. *Ibid.*
11. See Chapter II of this thesis.
12. Verrier Elwin, cited in Chapter II of this thesis.
13. Quoted in Nari K. Rustomji, *Verrier Elwin and India's North-Eastern Borderlands,* North-Eastern Hill University Publications, Shillong, 1988, pp. 58-59.
14. G. A. Smali to The Chairman, British Parliamentary Delegation, c/O Secretary, Information and Broadcasting, New Delhi, January 11, 1946 In G. N. Bardoloi Papers, Nehru Memorial Centre for Contemporary Studies, Manuscript Section, p. 7.
15. Nehru to B. Das, May 19, 1951, in S. Gopal, General Editor, *Selected Works of Jawaharlal Nehru,* Jawaharlal Nehru Memorial Fund, New Delhi, 1994 Vol. 16, Part I, p. 283.

16. Nehru to B. R. Medhi, August 1952, in S. Gopal, *ibid*. p. 199 (Foot Note No. 5).
17. S. Gopal, *Jawaharlal Nehru - A Biography*, Vol. 2, 1947-56, Oxford University Press, Delhi, 1983, p. 209.
18. *Ibid.*
19. *Ibid.*
20. Nehru, 'A Note on a Tour of the North-Eastern Frontier Areas' (19th October 1952 to October 1952,) this note was found in Elwin papers.
21. Nehru to Amrit Kaur, October 30, 1953, cited in S. Gopal, *Jawaharlal Nehru*, A Biography, Vol. 2, *op. cit.*, p. 209.
22. Elwin to T.N. Kaul, I.C.S., Joint Secretary to the Government of India, Ministery of External Affairs, New Delhi, December 12, 1953, File No. ATA/C/6 Listed as 8/88, Elwin Papers.
23. File No. ATA/T/2, Listed as File No. 133, pp. 71-72 in Elwin Papers.
24. I found this document in the Archives maintained by Talom Rukbo, a prominent cultural leader and the vanguard of the movement for DonyiPoloism in the present form.
25. *Ibid.*, p. 1.
26. *Ibid.*, pp. 1-2.
27. *Ibid.*, p. 3.
28. *Ibid.*
29. *Ibid.*, p. 3.
30. *Ibid.*, pp. 3-5.
31. *Ibid.*, pp. 6-7.
32. *Ibid.*, p. 8.
33. *Ibid.*, pp, 9-10.
34. *Ibid.*, p, 10.
35. See Verrier Elwin, *Democracy in NEFA*, Shillong, 1965.
36. Atul Chander Talukdar, *Political Transition in the Grassroots in Tribal India*, Omson Publications, New Delhi, 1987, pp. 49-51.
37. Reported in *NCCR*, Vol. XCVI, No. 5, May 1976, p. 309.
38. T. Koyu, Secretary, Adi Cultural and Literary Society, Pasighat to the Additional Deputy Commissioner, Pasighat, Letter No.

ACLS-7/76-77 Dated Pasighat the 9th June, 1977, File No. ACLS-7/76-77, Office of the Adi Cultural and Literary Society, Pasighat.

39. Letter No ACLS/1/76-77, May 23, 1977, File No. ACLS/76-77, Office of The Adi Cultural and Literary Society, Pasighat.

40. *Ibid.*, p. 55.

41. *Ibid.*

42. News Report in *NCCR*, Vol. XCIX, No. 2, February 1979, pp. 111-112.

43. See *NCCR*, Vol. XCVI, May, 1976, p. 309.

44. Reported in *NCCR*, vol. XCVI, No. 8 August 1976, p. 438.

45. P. K. Thungon, the then Chief Minister of Arunachal Pradesh. He made this Statement on the occasion of discussion on Arunachal Pradesh Freedom of Indigeneous Faith Bill, 1978 held in Arunachal Pradesh Legislative Assembly on 17, 18 and 19th. May 1978, in *Official Report*, Proceedings of the Arunachal Pradesh First Legislative Assembly, Second Session, 17, 18 and 19th May 1978, Assembly Secretariat, Arunachal Pradesh Nahar Lagun, p. 131. Now-on-wards Mentioned as *Official Report*, 1978.

46. "Introduction of Panchayat Raj Regulation 1967 in NEFA had provided for the Agency-Council-an apex body institution at the territory level as an administrative arrangement, without making any constitutional change. The Agency Council functioned for about four years from 3rd. December 1969 to August 1, 1972." -Sanjay Dubey, *Dynamics of Tribal Local Polity and Panchayat Raj in Arunachal Pradesh*, (Premier Publishing House, New Delhi, 1998, p. 66.).

47. *Ibid.*, p. 6, 21.

48. *Official Report*, 1978, *op. cit.*, p. 78.

49. *Ibid.*, p. 132.

50. *Ibid.*, p. 78.

51. *ibid:*, p. 132.

52. *Ibid.*, pp. 131-39.

53. *NCCR*, Vol. XCIX, No. 2, February 1979, p. 111.

54. *Ibid.*
55. *Ibid.*
56. *Ibid.*, p. 111.
57. *Ibid.*, p. 112.
58. *Ibid.*, p. 112.
59. *Ibid.*, p. 112.
60. Memorandum submitted to Shri Neelam Sanjiva Reddy, President of India by the People of Arunachal Pradesh in File No. 25, 1977-78, Adi Cultural and Literary Society, Pasighat, p. 8.
61. *Ibid.*
62. Reported in *NCCR*, Vol. XCVIII, No. 9, September, 1978, p. 462. (News column : 'News From Many Quarters', India).
63. *Ibid.*
64. *Ibid.*, p. 462.
65. *Ibid.*
66. Letter dated 18-8-78, File No. 25, 1977-78, Talom Rukbo's Archives.
67. T. Koyu, Secretary, Adi Cultural and Literary Society, Pasighat to the President of India, August 26, 1978, File No. ACLS-25/77-78, Archives of the Adi Cultural and Literary Society, Pasighat, (p. No. 8).
68. Shri T. Koyu, Secretary to Shri K. A. Raja, Lt. Governor, Government of Arunachal Pradesh, Itanager, No. ACLS-25/77-78, August 27, 1978, File No. ACLS-77/78, pp. 3-4.
69. *Ibid.*
70. T. Koyu to The Secretary, Social and Cultural Affairs, Along, Roying, Ziro and Bomdila, No. ACLS-25/77-78, September 16, 1978, p. 9.
71. *Ibid.*
72. *The Hindu*, September 18, 1978.
73. *Ibid.*
74. *Ibid.*
75. *Ibid.*
76. *Ibid.*

77. Doi Ado, Secretary, District Social Welfare Cultural Society, Siang District Along to the Secretary, Adi Cultural and Literary Society, Pasighat, No. SC/SWCS/ 23/78-79/11, September 26, 1978 in File No. 25, 1977-78, Adi Cultural and Literary Society, Pasighat.
78. 'A Brief Report of Special Bharat Darshan Tour of 6 (six) Members During the month of August and September 78' in Talom Rukbo's Archive.
79. *The Arunachal Pradesh Code*, vol. 111, Acts made by the Arunachal Pradesh Legislative Assembly, Government of Arunachal Pradesh Law and Judicial Department, Itanager, 1982, pp. 7-9.
80. *Ibid.*, p. 8.
81. Memo No. J-403 dated November 8, 1979 in File No. ACLS-7/85-86 Adi Cultural and Literary Society, Pasighat.
82. NCCR, Vol. XCIX, Nos 6-7, June-July, 1979, p. 361.
83. 'Sunrise or Sunset in Arunachal', *NCCR*, *op. cit.*, p. 362.
84. *Ibid.*, p. 370.
85. *NCCR*, Vol. CIVI, No. 7, August 1984, p. 369.
86. Reported in *NCCR*, Vol. C, No. 3, March 1980, p. 154.

Chapter - 5
Movement for Cultural Identity

I

CULTURAL AND LITERARY SOCIETIES

The indigeneous leaders started resorting to defence of their cultural practices as a result of perceived threat to the tribal cultural identity. Formation of Associations, especially cultural and literary Associations formed an important aspect of this agenda for cultural defence.[1] The Adis and Khamptis were the first to form such Associations. 'The Adi Cultural and Literary Society' was formally inaugurated at Along, the district headquarters of Siang, "with a two-day programme on 14th and 15th November 1971."[2] Simultaneously Adi Cultural and Literary society was formed at Pasighat.[3] The most important aims and objectives of these societies have been the preservation of traditional cultural heritage. Oshong Ering a prominent intellectual has explained it very succinctly. He was born on February 1, 1938 and belongs to Minyong sub-tribe of Adis. He received his earlier education at Sadiya and Pasighat and was sent to Shillong for Higher Education. After having completed his education he joined NEFA administration as area superintendent. In due course of time he was nominated to I.A.S. Cadre and after retirement he settled at Mirku village near Pasighat. He has been a prolific writer and been contributing articles on economic, political and cultural aspects of the tribes of Arunachal Pradesh to various journals and newspapers.

Thus he wrote in 1976 :

> Approximately three decades ago, Arunachal was brought under modern administrative system and life. Since then the people of the tribes came into closer contact with the people of outside world. People representing different communities came as administrators, Technicians, Teachers, and workers and they have infused new ideas and ideologies in the minds of the tribes. Being enthused with new cultural ideas or awakening, the people of the tribes have advanced in various fields. But in the midst of enthusiasm, there is every likelihood of paying less attention to the traditional culture of the people. The youth of the tribes have been dragged on to the storm of modern cultural ideas and at the same time, the older group of people are gradually dying out. *There is a tendency of burying traditional culture in oblivion. In course of time, our cultural traditions may fade away...and along with it may go our crafts, arts, dress., dances.* This will mean a genuine loss to the tribes and posterity will blame us for lack of wisdom and gross negligence.[4]

Presenting the report of the activities of the Adi cultural and Literary society, the Secretary of the Society, Talom Rukbo, pointed out the prevalence of two trends : (*a*) party politics, and (*b*) alien culture, are eroding the traditional culture and thus affecting the cultural identify of the people of Arunachal Pradesh.[5] Therefore, the alternative for them was to preserve their traditional culture.[6] Oshong Ering explains the meaning of traditional cultural heritage. By it he means belief systems, superstitious practices, myths, religious ethics, philosophy, rituals, songs, dances etc. transmitted from one generation to the next.[7] This is how the past has been used by the Adi intellectuals, in search for their identity. One may, recall, here, Prof. Romila Thapar's remarks on the interpretation of ancient Indian history "History has often been used in the search for an identity. Each contemporary group seeks its own identity in the past."[8] Thus Oshong Ering believes that through cultural traditions the people feel a sense of pride in their past and maintain their self-respect and dignity.[9] In fact, the intellectuals were aware of the fact that their folklores, myths etc. were not only important for sustaining their identity but also a great source of their cultural history.[10] Therefore, they felt it the utmost need to record the oral traditions. Tumpak Ete has thrown some light on this aspect. He was born in 1936 (approximate year) and belongs to Galong sub-tribe of the Adis. He had been an active social worker and been writing on various aspects of the Adi Society. Compiling the sacred lores of the Adis, he points out :

> With the conditions coming in and cracking the old structure of the society, these myths are likely to either get modified or lose their validity, but they are not likely to lose their value as a means of getting an insight into the mind and as material for sociological and literary study.[11]

Again, he remarks :

> With the spread of modern School education which takes children away from the traditional education and way of life,. the priestly school of rhapsodists is fast disappearing. The old tales are losing their appeal because of ignorance of their real purpose and new ideas of social order and function. So their is every reason to fear that if these are not written down now, they will be lost forever. Soon there would be none who would know these lengthy narratives. This fear oppressed me and I decided to devote myself entirely to the task of preservation of this valuable heritage of ours.[12]

In this respect Sudhir Kakar's ideas on the myths as the repository of a distrinctive cultural identity are relevant for our study. "Among the various manifestations of any culture," says he, "myths in their classical form, or popularized and bowdlerized in legends and folk tales, occupy a special niche of honour...They can be read as a kind of collective historical conscience, instructions from venerable ancestors on 'right' and 'wrong', which serves to bind the members of a group to each other and thus to forge a collective identity, separate and distinct from the collective identities of other groups."[13]

II

LITERARY INTELLECTUALS AND CULTURAL IDENTITY

The Adi intellectuals felt the need to develop Adi (common for all the sub-tribes) language and literature and a suitable script for it.[14] It led to the formation of Adi Agom Kebang (Adi Sahitya Sabha) on November 12, 1981. Talom Rukbo a leading literary personality and vanguard of the cultural movement among the Adi groups was one of the prominent founding members of this organisation. He was born on October 30, 1938 in Kalek village of East Siang district. He belongs to the Pasi community, a sub-tribe of the Adis. His father, late Shri Rukpaying Rukbo was a *Gambura*. Talom Rukbo received his earlier education at Sadiya and Pasighat and higher education at Shillong. He joined government service in 1961 as Language officer in NEFA administration later on he was appointed as Special officer (culture) and posted at Pasighat. But the Government job was incompatible with the artist in him. His artistic temperament must have felt stifled by the mechanical and routine duties a Government servant has to discharge. The creativity within him must have been making him, restive with his job and was not getting any opportunity to gush out. Therefore in order to give free rein to his creativity and also devote time to the social activity he resigned from the Government service in 1976.

Talom Rukbo has written a large number of poems, compiled Abangs (sacred-lores) and folk songs. Literature for him has been an important weapon for forging cultural identity among the Adis. One of his most popular poems titled "Kaaboma-Kaaboma, Ami Ati Kaaboma" (No temptation, No temptation of others' things) weaves the theme of cultural rootedness and resistance to the dominance of other cultures. To quote it :

Kaaboma Kaaboma
Ami ati Kaaboma

Yaaike o.e. Kaaboma
opan dokom Kaaboma

Mamike ome Kaaboma
Are dokom Kaaboma
Ami ati Kaaboma

Kaaboma ... ...
Ami ati ... ...

Kenma dokom Kaaboma
Nokke Lenko eding dung
Ane Lering eding dung
Ami ati Kaaboma

Kaaboma ... ...
Ami ati ... ...

Mide dokom Kaaboma
Yaaike nitom Kensila
Yao dokom Kaaboma
Mamoke orman geepala
Ami ati Kaaboma

Kaaboma ... ...
Ami ati ... ...

Mikma dokom Kaaboma
Ami Yatkol tatlangi
Nyoma dokom Kaaboma
Ami nomkol tatlangi
Ami ati Kaaboma

Kaaboma ... ...
Ami ati ... ...

Dite katan Kamp Kaaboma
Sine tattan tatpo tatoma
Katan Kampo Kaaboma
Tattan Tatpo tatboma

Ami ati Kaaboma

Kaaboma ... ...
Ami ati ... ...[15]

(To sum up the gist of the poem in a few words :" I may be poor, illiterate, rustic, naive, inarticulate but I have no temptation for other things and cannot be allured. I know all that glitters is not gold. My parents' and my own roots are very strong and therefore I need not pine for others' belonging.)

In fact, the theme of cultural rootedness and a feeling of a sense of pride in his own culture runs through many of Talom Rukbo's poems. Thus in the poem "Turmona Yelot" (My culture enlivens me")[16] Talom Rukbo glorifies his culture and states that he derives nourishment from his culture :

Ngem turmona Yelot
Matokom Mapamang
Tani giidnag se
Yaayi maameke baddaklok
Lembomnem Yelot
Sekena turmona bedang.

(My culture enlivens me and I won't find it anywhere. Right from my childhood I derived nourishment from my culture.)

The poet states that he would like to nurture his children also in this culture :

Ngom turmona yelot
Ane ayume mii yum Sila
Abu angame mingam Sila
Ome Kulungem Kinape
Oo Selongem Sonape
Aaji Selongem Sonape
Niilum erangg aabe lok.

II (b)

Talom Rukbo's literary expression of cultural identity in the form of cultural defence must not be read as a traditionalist response to modernity, rather it is a manifestation of modernity itself. "True modernity" writes Partha Chatterjee "consists in determining the particular forms of modernity that are suitable in particular circumstances, that is, applying the methods of reason to identify or invent the specific technolgies of modernity that are appropriate for our purposes."[17] This ideal of modernity, that involves defence of cultural practices accompanying the economic fruits of development is represented in Prof. Tamo Mibang's poems.[18] Thus in the poem 'Bulsi' (repentance) the poet seems to welcome the urbanisation and concomitant economic development. But in another poem 'illusion' he seems to be wary of the values brought about by development. Through a contrast between a native man and an outsider, former representing nature and the later civilization, the poet brings out the conflict between two different cultures. He would welcome the outsider provided he adapts itself to nature. Similarly in the poem 'prayer' the poet welcomes the modern knowledge which is symbol of civilization but at the same time wants to avoid the negative aspects of civilization. ('Dusty and infectious wind, infect me not').

Conflict between nature and civilization is the pivotal theme around which the plot of Lummer Dai's novel *Prithvibir Hanhi* (The Earth Smiles) is weaved. Lummer Dai (norn on June 1, 1940) belongs to the Dai clan of Pasis, a sub-tribe of the Adis. He received his earlier education at Pasighat (now the headquarters of East-Siang district) and was sent to Shillong and Guwahati for higher education. After completing education, he joined government service and retired from the post of Director, Department of Information and Publicity, Government of Arunachal Pradesh. His interest in writing on various cultural aspects of his society goes back to his school days at Pasighat. His literary production (authored four novels) is *Pahar Hile Hile, Prithbi Hanhi Hanhi* (The Earth Smiles, 1963) *Mon Aur Mon* (1966) and *Konyar Mulya* (The Bride-Price, 1978). All of these fictional narratives were written in Assamese language and script. Lummer Dai adopted realism as a form in his fictional narratives. Therefore, it is worthwhile to explore in general, the relationship between literary production and social reality in the following section.

II (c)

A novelist following realism as a mode represents "the true essence of reality" in his fictional narratives. The "true essence of reality" has to be distinguished from "photographic reality or naturalism." Explaining the later, John Somervile writes :

> Photographic realism or naturalism in the realm of art is analogous to what formal logic is in the realm of Science, or mechanistic materialism is in the field of philosophy. It fails to see things what they are being transformed into. It transfixes reality, and in so doing, devitalises and kills it. It accumulates minute details, but discerns no patterns, sees no forest, only tress; no whole, only fragmentary parts. It is blindly empirical, fruitlessly static.[20]

The 'true essence of reality', therefore, is an exploration of the "essential forces hidden behind the appearances",[21] or in the words of Brecht, a penetration to the causal nexus in the society.[22] It is a dramatisation of a process.[23] It is presented in the form of historically significant social and ideological trends. These trends are represented by portraying the typical characters. A typical character is one "in whom particular traits are combined with a high level of generalization."[24] Thus Falstaff (in Shakespeare), Don Quixote (in Cervantes), Tom Jones (in Fielding) are all types, but they "are types in whom the social characteristics constantly reveal the individual and in whom personal hopes, hungers, loves, jealousies and ambitions in turn light up the social background."[25]

An individual with strong, positive values comes in conflict with a society which either condemns or allows little possibility for the expression of those values. There is a dialectical interaction between such an individual and the objective social reality and out of struggle between the values represented by that individual and that of society, between the old order and the new, emerges the new order.[26] But this new order retains at the same time the characteristics of the old order, too[27], and this creates certain ambiguity or contradiction within the individual. This is an important dimension of Lummer Dai's creative universe.

The question whether reality depicted in literature coincides with the objective nature of reality has been the subject of considerable attention. What is at the centre of this discussion is the nature and limitations of the autonomy of art in relation to the reality which forms its source. Bertold Brecht points out" A work which does not exhibit its sovereignty *vis-a-vis* reality is not a work of art.[28] But at the same time the world represented in a literary work is not merely a world of fantasy and illusion. It contain "nothing that does not also exist in the given reality, the actions, thoughts, feelings and dreams of men and women."[29]

The literary work, according to Piere Macherey "must be studied in double perspective : in relation to history, and in relation to an ideological version of that history."[30] And moreover, a historical period "does not spontaneously produce a single, monolithic ideology, but a series of ideologies determine by the total relation of forces; each ideology is shaped by the pressures upon the class which generates it."[31] For the philosopher Michel Foucault, the name for 'ideology'; is 'discourse'.[32] We also have been using the category 'discourse' instead of 'ideology' in this report.

II (d)

To revert to a brief discussion of Lummer Dai's novel *Prithvibir Hanhi* (The Earth smiles).

The plot of the novel revolves around the relationships between kardug, Karpung, Gachi, Liyi, Libo and Bankang. Gachi is beautiful, innocent, honest girl. She has all the finer qualities of a tribal girl. Libo is straightforward, innocent, naive, tribal boy. These two characters are ascribed all the values associated with nature. Kardung is a cunning, speculative, self-seeking, deceptive person who is the son of a rich man. He visits Dibrugarh regularly in connection with business. He has been attributed with all the negative features of a commercial society, in other words, of civilization. Libo and Gachi are not affected by the debilitating effects of civilization. Kardug takes Libo to Dibrugarh and steals not only his money but also deserts him. Though the writer might not have any sympathy for Kardung but he emerges as the most fascinating character. Here the text itself defeats writers's intentions. Since Lummer Dai has adopted realism as a form he had to conform to the reality principle and thus kardug emerges as a future man. Perhaps the writer could read into the future and visualise the process in which the society would move as result of the structural changes in the society. The story of the novel ends without providing any solution. Perhaps he had no solution to offer to this complex issue. But the solutions are not important. The significance of the novel lies in the manner Lummer Dai has posed certain questions. These questions are : *(a)* in what direction the tribal society is moving and *(b)* what would be the nature of Adis' cultural identity faced with the intrusion of new value system and destruction of "a whole way of life."[33] He leaves the reader disturbed, though without any definite answer to the questions he has raised.

III

REFORMATION OF POPULAR CULTURAL PRACTICES

Reformation of popular cultural practices has been another mark of new cultural identity of the educated social group. By appropriating popular/tribal culture this group has been exercising its own hegemony over the rest of the society. Thus cultural identity also involves the question of empowerment.

The cultural practices which are not suitable for the contemporary needs of the society are rejected and sought to be eliminated in the name of 'social evils'. Some of these practices are : bride-price, child-marriage, forced marriage, polygamy, excessive sacrifice of animals etc. Thus, tradition becomes a selective process. Whatever is suitable for existing needs of the society is appropriated from the past and is passed on as tradition. The tradition thus gets invented and 'grafted on the old'.[34]

Thus sacrifice has been an important aspect of tribal cultural practice. Most of their rites and rituals revolve around sacrifice of animals. But the intellectuals have been trying to bring about reform in this aspect. Thus Prof. Tamo Mibang feels that the practice of sacrifice of the mithuns, pigs etc. can be retained only on the occasions of festivals since it forms an important tradition but it should be confined to a very limited scale and it must be completely banned on other occasions.[35] But Oshong Ering recommends total ban on the sacrifice of animals even on the occasion of the festivals. He believes "there are certain traditions which need not require preservation and revitalization,"[36] and killing of animals forms one of these traditions which do not require preservation. Since he does not want to discourage the spirit of sacrifice, therefore he suggests some symbolic image as an alternative to killing the animal. He suggests "carving of huge wooden images of mithuns with wheel," and this "can be rolled out" on the occasion.[37] Lummer Dai feels that "without sacrifice also deities can be worshipped by offering *Apong* and rice, rice-powder etc."[38]

IV

CHILD-MARRIAGE, FORCED-MARRIAGE, AND BRIDE-PRICE

Child-marriage, forced-marriage and bride-price (all the three interconnected) have been the 'social-evils' which the intellectuals among the Adi tribe have been trying to eliminate from their society. All these practices mainly affected the women in the society. It is the male intellectuals who first of all took up issues affecting women. "Patriarchal systems offer women few opportunities until men decide it is time for change."[39]

The marriage payments, in general, have been linked with various issues : *(a)* status and the economic contribution of brides to the groom's family;[40] nature of residence and inheritance system;[41] shortage of potential brides and bridegrooms;[42] tendency towards egalitarianism or stratification in a given society.[43] There payments have been discussed within the broad categories : bride-price, dowry, groom-wealth, bride-service, and indirect dowry.[44]

Bride-price marriages have been interpreted variously.[45] This literature can be broadly categorised into two groups : *(a)* economic interpretation and *(b)* kinship relations. The lack of space does not permit us to discuss this literature in detail.

Among the Galo-Adis, the community forming he background of Lummer Dai's novel, *Konyar-Mulya*, the system of bride-price has been prevailing for centuries together.[46] Linked with it is the system of child-marriage. "Sometimes", says Tai Nyori, "even a small girl is married to an aged man or a grown up girl is married to a small boy."[47] Gamli Padu delineates another aspect of the system of child-marriage, known as *Nappe-nyida*. In this system "Before the birth of their children two friends (Kadens) come to understand that after birth, "if one's child is a daughter and that of the other is a son, their marriage should be solemnised between them".[48] In case of violation of such marriages by a boy or a girl when he or she grows up, the case is settled by the Kebangs.[49]

Lummer Dai has dealt with this theme in his novel *Konyar-Mulya* very effectively. It is, therefore, worthwhile to narrate in brief the dominant narrative of this novel.

Gumba, the protagonist of the main narrative of this novel, was married during her childhood when she was not more than three years of age. Her 'so called husband' was at that time about ten years of age. She was "carried" to groom's house by here mother on here back. Kargum, Gumba's father had received the bride-price for her marriage.[50] After that when she grew up Kargum admitted her in school when he "saw others send their children" to school. When she was studying in class XII Kargum decided to send her to her in-laws house. Gumba was shocked on hearing that she was 'sold' during her childhood. She declared to her father "better to kill me than to sell to somebody." She asserted "you may send my body as a bundle, but not my mind." The family members of Kargum remained in a tense state as she remained steadfast in her refusal to accept this marriage. However after normalcy in the surface came back to the family, Gumba went back to the school.

In the meanwhile a rumour was circulated by her in-laws' family that Gumba loved some boy in the school and she refused to go to her husband. Therefore, the clan-members of the family decided to call Kebang and Kargum was summoned to appear before the Kebang along with his daughter. Gumba refused to comply with this order and her father had to appear before the Kebang alone on the appointed day. He did not object to the Kebang's decision that Gumba be dragged from her school to her in-laws' house. He, therefore, accompanied Mindak (Gumba's father-in-law) and his clan members to the town-school. On her refusal to go with them the clan members of her father-in-law dragged her forcibly inspite of her resistance. The crowd simply kept on looking at her.[51] On the way Gumba hardened her mind and was determined to face all sorts of tortures "that might be inflicted on her" and not surrender under any circumstances. On reaching their house she refused to take food and even a drop of water. The youths bound her hand and feet and dragged her to Dakto's (her husband) bed and tied her body with the bed in lying position.[52] But Gumba resisted all the attempts made by her husband to "gratify himself" and "in an utmost attempt to protect herself" she gave a "a forceful blow with her bound hands on Dakto's face."[53] As a result he got hurt. Next morning she was put in a dark cell in the *tungu.* Even in the cell she refused to take food and water and after sixteen days of fast when she was on the verge of death her in-laws took her to her parents house. She was administered Jack fruit and gradually brought back to consciousness and within a few days regained her strength. Her father decided to return her bride-price and *Bango-Kebang* was called which decided the case in her favour and she was released.

IV (b)

Lummer Dai has represented Gumba not only as a victim of the social system but also has invested her with an agency which impels her to struggle against patriarchy. She resists male violence with the weapons of the weak by resorting to fast unto death.[54] The author was faced with a dilemma whether to conclude the narrative with Gumba's death in the cell.[55] Seeing him restless for three days his wife suggested that Gumba must be made to remain alive so as to set an example to the struggling women folk.[56] And therefore, Lummer Dai prolonged the narrative.

Gumba's agency provides a critique of 'commonsense.'[57] The idea of 'common-sense' is to be understood not in its everyday usage, but as "the conception of the world which is uncritically absorbed by the various social and cultural environments in which the moral individuality of the average man is developed."[58] It is "the spontaneous philosophy of the multitude."[59] It is a conception of the world with which the subordinate classes rationalize their place in the world. Her struggle against male violence interpellates us. Interpellation explains how the lure of the narrative unconsciously gathers readers into the value-system, beliefs and ideology of the narrator.[60]

The dominant discourse in this narrative is that of modernity. And "there is no promised land of modernity" says Partha Chatterjee, "outside the network of power."[61] Gumba's education invests her with a sense of power. That the emerging educated class had been developing a new sense of power and was responsible for bringing about key changes in the society, has been discussed in chapter 3. Two of the marginal narratives in *Konyar Mulya* throw some light on this "network of power." Gumba was summoned by her father to visit them for an urgent work. (He had decided to send her to her in-laws house). Her childhood friends came to know of her arrival from the town and they came to see her. Their conversation with her brings out the 'cultural distinction' between Gumba and her friends. They started cursing their own life which they believed was full of drudgery revolving around production and reproduction.[62] But the discussion continues only for a brief time and her father requests them to allow her to take some rest. She could not sleep at night because of "mental agony" when she came to know that she was 'sold' during her childhood. Therefore, she "took the paddy in a winnow and began to husk in the pestly."[63] The sound of paddy husking awakened Gumba's two sisters-in-law. Both of them came from their beds and came near Gumba. Their conversation with her is very significant from our point of view :

> "You need not husk paddy, Yaba," said her elder sister-in-law in a loving tone, "why, sister?" Gumba asked.
>
> "Your soft and pointed fingers will become rough and blunt. Then you won't be able to write good hand-writing. See ours", she showed her palm and then continued, "these are rough, cracked and blunt."[64]

The author does not delve into the details but these very brief conversations are symbolically very significant in understanding the emerging "social distinction" in the society. Why Lummer Dai refers to this "social distinction" obliquely? It is 'problematic of a text'. The problematic of a text "relates to its moment of historical existence as much by what it excludes as by what it includes."[65] That is to say, it encourages a "text to answer questions posed by itself, but at the same time it generates the production of 'deformed' answers to the question which it attempts to exclude."[66] Thus a problematic is "structured as much by what is absent (what is not said) as by what is present (what is said). The task of critical practice is to deconstruct the text (read it symptomatically) to reveal the workings of its problematic and thus establish its relationship to its historical conditions of existence."[67] Pierre Machery further develops this argument. For him, the text is a construction with a multiplicity of meanings.[68] All fictional texts are 'decentred' in the "specific sense in that they consist of a confrontation between several discourses : explicit, implicit, silent and absent.[69] Machery contends that "that in order for something to be said, other things must be left unsaid."[70] It is the reasons for these absences, these silences, within a text which must be interrogated. "What is important in the work is what it does not say."[71] To explain a text, it is necessary to go beyond it, to understand what it "is compelled to say in order to say what it wants to say."[72] It is here that the text's 'unconscious' is constituted. And it is a text's 'unconscious' that "its relationship to the ideological and historical conditions of its existence is revealed. It is here ,in the absent centre, hollowed out by conflicting discourses, that the text is related to history."[73]

Cultural hegemony and its reproduction is implicit in the new public spaces created by the educated classes. The members of the youth club in *Konyar-Mulya* organised a cultural show in honour of Deputy-Commissioner when he paid a visit to Kargum's village. It was a theatrical performance by a group of young boys and girls on the evils of child-marriage and bride-price. The musical instruments used for the song were "harmonium and tabla'.[74] part of an alien culture in the context of the Adis. This narrative symbolically represents 'mainstream' cultural hegemony. The presence of the representative of the Indian state here is not accidental, it forms part of the larger context where the State appropriated even the public spaces in Arunachal Pradesh.

But Lummer Dai did not accept this hegemony passively. It is rather contested. A very important site of contestation of this hegemony in *Konyar-Mulya* is that of community. This site becomes an arena of struggle between the emerging educated class and the village elders. It is also the site where the educated class creates an agenda of resistance against the State. The category of 'community' however, is a shifting one. "Community in a pre-capitalist culture" says Gyanendra Pandey "defines itself precisely by its *territoriality* and at the same time by its *temporality*.[75] In Arunachal it is based on clan, village, a group of villages, sub-tribe and tribe. In this novel the village community seems to be divided on the question of return of the bride-price.[76] The author does not take to Statist discourse on the question of customary laws/community, that is on the question of the emancipation of women *vis-a-vis* the customary laws. When Gumba was on fast the representatives of the student community and Adi women's society approached Kargum to save Gumba's life by paying back the bride-price and he showed his reluctance, the students threatened him to be arrested by the state authorities. But Kargum refused to be cowed down by these threats.[77] However, he requested the head Gam to call Bango Kebang to settle the question of return of the bride-price. Kargum took this decision when his daughter was brought home on her death-bed. The heated debate took place in the Kebang. The members of the youth club though not allowed to participate in the deliberations of the Kebang symbolically created an impact by their presence in the corner of the Hall. However, the scale was turned in favour of Gumba when Minjum, educated member of the Kebang, and a school-teacher by profession delivered a very persuasive speech about the validity of some of the customary practices in a changing society.[78] We are reminded here of the debate on Sati in colonial India in the 19th century. In the words of Lata Mani :

> Tradition was not the ground on which the status of women was being contested. Rather the reverse was true : women in fact became the site on which tradition was debated and reformulated.[79]

Therefore, in *Konyar Mulya* too, the tradition got reformulated in favour of the new emerging educated class.

V

WOMEN'S MOVEMENT

Any movement for cultural identity is incomplete without taking up the question of women's status in society. As discussed in the preceding section that an educated woman had to seek the support of the male section of the educated society to achieve her liberation from her forced-marriage propped up by customary-laws. But gradually the percentage of women's literacy had been increasing in Arunachal Pradesh. And it was being realized that struggle against perceived 'social evils' affecting the women folk, would have to be taken up by women themselves, and take up cudgels against injustice done to women. For this women started organising themselves first at the State level and subsequently at the district levels. They formed an association 'Arunachal Pradesh Women's Welfare Society, Itanagar' on Tenth October, One Thousand Nine Hundred Seventy Nine (October,, 10, 1979). The preamble of this Society reads as follows :

> We, the women of Arunachal Pradesh, have solemnly resolved to constitute 'Arunachal Pradesh Women's Welfare Society' in order to bring integration and foster understanding among all younger generation and thereby to bring about unity among the women of Arunachal Pradesh to exploit the energy of young spirit for the greater interest of all the women of Arunachal Pradesh and to preserve, promote and protect our culture and tradition and also to protect human rights among the women of Arunachal Pradesh and to drive out all forms of social evils and bad practices from our society and thereby, to bring a *New Light* for women in Arunachal Pradesh, do herby enact this constitution for the Arunachal Pradesh Womens Welfare Society, this day of Tenth October, One Thousand Nine Hundred Seventy Nine.[80]

Inculcation of awareness was one of the prime objectives of this society, especially about some of the cultural practices :

> to act as an organization to ensure the security, expansion and development of indigeneous women of Arunachal Pradesh and thereby, promoting them in social values of women of Arunachal Pradesh by educating them to discard the social evils of the traditional customs which is a hindrance to their interest in the changed circumstances of the social life of this day.[81]

Simultaneously Society's branches were opened in various districts of Arunachal Pradesh. In the Adi areas also its branch was opened at Along. Women's Welfare Society, Along, in 1979. The society has been taking various issues affecting women. Some of these are :

(a) violence against women and children.

(b) Cases related to child-marriage, forced-marriage, incompatible marriages and bride-price.

(c) Issues related to widows.

(d) Cases related to desertion of wives and maintenance.

Thus, the various public spaces created by educated men and women have become the sites of resistance against the 'mainstream' cultural hegemony as well as exercising the hegemony of the new educated class over the rest of the society.

REFERENCES

1. These associations have been registered and are listed in general file No. SR/ITA, Arunachal Pradesh Secretariat, Political Department.
2. Jayanta Kumar Sarkar, 'Development of Identity Consciousness in Arunachal Pradesh' in K.S. Singh, ed., *Tribal Movements in India*, Vol. 1, Delhi, 1980, p. 234.
3. Listed in general file No. SR/ITA, *op.cit.*
4. Oshong Ering, *'Preservation and Revitalization of Cultural Heritage of Arunachal Pradesh,* Adi Cultural and Literary Society, Pasighat, November, 1976, p. 5. Emphasis mine.
5. *Echo*, 19 June, 1987, p. 3; also see Talom Rukbo's poem 'Election Kiiruk' (election campaign). This poem was read on the occasion of *Adi Abong Kebang* conference held at Bolang on January 6, 1989. The poet remonstrates that the party politics has brought about disunity in the society.
6. *Echo*, June 19, 1987, p. 3. The Adi Literary and Cultural Society at this conference decided to open cultural societies in every *bango* of East Siang district, which would help Adi cultural and Literary society in its task of strengthening cultural activities. The other important suggestion included provision of compulsory classes of tribal culture with an inclusion of Miri, Ponung and Delong dance in every school of East Siang, active participation of younger generation in festival dances and improvement of dance dresses with colourful designs of original pattern.
7. *Op. cit.*, p. 5.
8. Romila Thapar, *The Past and Prejudice,* Delhi, 1975, p. 69.
9. *Op. cit.*, p. 8.
10. Tumpak Ete., *Nyibu Agom*, vol. i. p. 2.
11. *Ibid.*, p. 2.
12. *Ibid.*, Preface, p. 1.
13. Sudhir Kakar, The *Inner World : A Psycho-analytic Study of Childhood and Society in India*, 2nd. edition, (Delhi : Oxford University Press, 1981), p. 4.
14. See Chapter 7 of this book.
15. *Arshi* (Mirror). *Adi Cultural and Literary Society,* Pasighat,

August, 1990, pp. 23-24. One of my respondents informed me that it has been very popular song since 1980 among the Adi youths especially in Pasighat area.

16. This poem was written on 10-4-1984 and consists of 24 stanzas. I am grateful to Prof. Tamo Mibang for providing me the original manuscript and reading it to me and simultaneously translating it into English language.

17. Partha Chatterjee, Talking about our Modernity in Two Languages', in Partha Chatterjee, *A Possible India,* Essays in Political Criticism, (Delhi : Oxford University Press, 1997), p. 269.

18. The poems written by Prof. Tamo Mibang are : (i) Clarion Call, (2) Illusions, (3) Invisible Stranger, (4) Prayer, (5) Bulsi, (6) Ngo Turmona, (7) Reshape me, (8) Alak (Hand), (9) Ngok Agom (My Voice), (10) Kangkut Sila (Look Back).

19 This poem was published by Adi Abong Kebang (Adi Sahitya Sabha) as stated by the poet himself.

20. Quoted in Howard Fast, Literature and Reality, Mumbai, 1953, p. 54.

21. George Lukacs, 'Appearance and essence' in Gaylord C. Roy and Ursula Beitz, ed., *Preserva and Create,* New York, 1973, p. 8.

22. See Werner Mittenzwei, 'The Brecht-Lukacs Debate', in Gaylord Le Roy and Ursula Beitz, *Preserve and Create, op. cit.,* pp. 199-229.

23. Raymond Williams, 'Literature and Sociology', *New Left Review,* 67, May-June, 1971, p. 14.

24. Gaylord C. Le Roy and Ursula Beitz, *op. cit.*, p. 5.

25. Ralph Fox, *The Novel and the People,* Moscow, 1956, p. 66.

26. Here we may refer to the remarks made by Lucien Goldmann :

> For a dynamic thinker...whole of reality is a dynamic whole which progresses by the conflict between thesis and anti-thesis to a synthesis which both integrates and goes beyond them...this is the clearest possible expression of the dilemma : all human order is inadequate, and yet man must never give up his quest for adequate order.

...In Lucien Goldmann, *The Hidden God.* Translated by Philip Thody, London, 1964, pp. 194, 199.

27. As Ralph Fox points out "The changes take place, men become conscious of them, they 'fight out' the conflict between the old and new in their minds, but they do so unevenly; burdened by all kinds of past heritage, often unclearly, and always in such a way that it is not easy to trace the changes in men's minds." *op.cit.*, p. 62.
28. Quoted in Herbert Marcuse, *The Aesthetic Dimension*, towards a critique of Marxist Aesthetic, Boston, 1978, p. 32.
29. Herbet Marcuse, *ibid.*, p. 54.
30. Pierre Machery, *A Theory of Literary Production*, Translated from the French by Geoffrey Wall, Routledge and Kegan Paul, London, 1978, p. 115.
31. *Ibid.*
32. Cited in Jeremy Tambling *Narrative and Ideology*, Philadelphia, 1991, p. 47.
33. For the category 'Whole way of Life' see Raymond Williams, *Politics and Letters*, Interviews with New Left Review, NLB, London, 1970, p. 116.
34. For the concept 'invention of tradition' see Eric Hobsbawm, 'Introduction : Invention of Traditions', in Eric Hobsbawm and Terence Ranger, *The Invention of Tradition*, Cambridge University Press, Cambridge, 1983, pp. 1-14.
35. Personal Interview, April 10, 1998, Arunachal University Campus, Rono Hills, Doimukh.
36. Oshong Ering, *op. cit.*, p. 10.
37. *Ibid.*, p. 10.
38. Interview with Lummer Dai, Nahar Lagun, February 1, 1998.
39. Geraldine Forbes, *Women in Modern India*, The New Cambridge History of India, (New Delhi : Cambridge University Press, 1998, Reprint 1999), p. 6.
40. See Van Der Veen, K., *I Give Thee My Daughter*, Assen, 1972; S. Lidnerbaum, 'Implications for Women of Changing Marriage transactions in Bangladesh', *Studies in Family Planning*, 1981, 12 (11) : 394-401; all cited in Mohan Singh, 'Transition From Bride - Price to Dowry : Marriage Payments in a Rural North

Indian Area' *Man in India*, 77 (2 and 3) : June - September, 1997, p. 120.

41. M.E. Spiro, 'Marriage Payments : A Paradigm for the Burmese Perspective'. *Journal of Anthropological Research*, 1975, 31 (2) : 89-115; N. Yalman, *Under* the *Bo Tree*, Berkeley, 1967, all cited in Mohan Singh, *op. cit.*, p. 120.

42. J.C. Caldwell, P.H. Reddy and P. Caldwell, eds., 'The Causes of Marriage Change in South India', *Population Studies*, cited in Mohan Singh, *op. cit.*, p. 120.

43. J. Goody, 'Bride-Wealth and Dowry in Africa and Eurasia', in J. Goody and S.J. Tambiah, eds., *Bride-wealth and dowry*, Cambridge, 1973, pp. 1-58, cited in Mohan Singh, *op. cit.*, p. 120.

44. J. Goody, op. cit; M.E. Spiro, *op. cit*; J. Nash, "A Note on Groom-price", *American Anthropologist*, 1978, 80 (1) : 101-108; A. Schlegel and E. Eloul, " Marriage Transactions : Labour, Property, Status', *American Anthropologists*, 1988,90 (2) : 291-309.

45. See Mohan Singh, *op. cit.*, pp. 119-41; Nancy Tapper, 'Direct Exchange And Bride-Price : Alternative Forms in A Complex Marriage System", *Man*, Vol. 16, 1981, pp. 387-407; Valerio Valeri, 'Buying Women But Not Selling Them : Gift And Commodity Exchange In Huaulu Alliance' *Man* Vol. 29, No. 1, March, 1992, pp. 1-26; Abha Chauhan, *Tribal Women and Social Change in India*, Eatwah, 1990; M. P. Jagirdar, 'Status of Women' A Case Study with special reference to North Eastern Region' in *Tribal Women and Development*, Agenda Papers, 1981 cited in Abha Chauhan, *op. cit*; P. K. Misra, 'From Bride-Price to Dowry' in K. S. Singh, ed., *Economies of the Tribes and Their Transformation*, New Delhi, 1984; besides see the literature cited in foot-notes 40-44 above in this chapter.

46. Tai Nyori, *History and Culture of The Adis*, New Delhi, 1993, p. 210.

47. *Ibid.*, p. 210.

48. Gamli Padu, 'Neppe-Nyida', *Arunachal News*, April-May, 1982, pp. 34-35.

49. Oshong Ering, 'Child-marriage in **Adi** Society and Plight of girls' ***Arunachal News*, August, 1981, pp.** 9-12.

50. Lummer Dai, *Bride*-Price, English translation of *Konyar-Mulya*, translated from Assamese to English by Jogendra Nath, Himalaya Publishers, New Delhi, 1994, p. 2. All the references cited here are from this edition of the novel in English.
51. *Ibid.*, p. 51.
52. *Ibid.*, p. 56.
53. *Ibid.*
54. *Ibid.*, pp. 55-60, 59-70, 80-83, 84-95.
55. Interview with Lummer Dai and his wife, Naharlagun, February 1, 1998.
56. *Ibid.*
57. The concept of 'common-sense' has been derived from Antonio Gramsci, *Selections from the Prison Notebooks, op. cit.*, pp. 323-33, 419-425.
58. *Ibid.*, p. 419.
59. *Ibid.*, p. 421.
60. For the concept 'interpellation' see chapter 2 of this book.
61. Partha Chatterjee, *op. cit.*, p. 280.
62. *Bride-Price, op. cit.*, pp. 8-9.
63. *Ibid.*, p. 16.
64. *Ibid.* p. 16.
65. Louis Althusser, cited in John Storey, *op. cit.*, p. 30..
66. *Ibid.*
67. *Ibid.*
68. Pierre Machery, cited in John Storey, *op. cit.*, p. 31.
69. *Ibid.*
70. *Ibid.*, p. 32.
71. *Ibid.*
72. *Ibid.*, p. 33.
73. *Ibid.*
74. *Bride-Price*, pp. 40-44.

75. Gyanendra Pandey, 'Community as History' in Gyanendra Pandy, *The Construction of Communalism in Colonial North India*, (Delhi : Oxford University Press, 1994), First Published in 1990, p. 110.
76. *Bride-Price*, pp. 109-114.
77. *Ibid.*, pp. 79-83.
78. *Ibid.*, pp. 115-127.
79. Lata Mani, 'Contentious Traditions : The Debate on Sati in Colonial India' in Kum Kum Sangari and Sudesh vaid, eds. *Recasting Women : Essays in Colonial History*, Kali For Women, 1989, pp. 117-118.
80. Preamble in *By-Laws and Constitution of Arunachal Pradesh Women's Welfare Society*, p. 1.
81. *Ibid.*

Chapter - 6
Movement for Indigeneous Religious Identity

I

OFFICIAL DISCOURSE ON INDIGENOUS RELIGION

Promotion of tribal religion formed an important aspect of the agenda of exercising cultural hegemony on the part of the officials of the Indian State while formulating the cultural policies in NEFA/Arunachal Pradesh :

> The People's religious beliefs are to respected and sympathetically understood and on no account are any efforts to be made to draw them into the rituals and faith of another religion.[1]

The policy-makers believed that the tribal religion :

> may survive *as it is*, provided the official attitude becomes one of respect for it and provided also senior officers show a kind of official patronage to the tribal religious functions.[2]

However, it was at the same time felt to be insufficient to "meet the spiritual needs of a changing situation."[3] "The old basic religion" may not be able to "meet situations" arising out of "stoppage of such practices as head-hunting or introduction of modern medicines."[4] Therefore the policy-makers were in favour of developing it by providing state patronage.[5] K.L. Mehta states :

> We may well have to create a class of modern tribal priests,

who could pass the message of the reformed religion, as it were, to the educated tribals as they grow up in schools.[6]

It was felt to "provide a climate in which the old religions can grow and reform themselves from within *so that ultimately there will be in NEFA religious concepts that will be truly tribal in character,* yet having a wider view and a purer conception of God and man."[7] The following Directives were given to the officials for providing a proper 'climate.' :

(i) The first is that we should study and try to understand the religions of the areas we live. This is not only a fascinating pastime but, if it is done with tact and sincerity, will in itself help to encourage the tribal people in their faith. Besides, the very fact that we take such interest helps to cure the inferiority complex that so easily arises.[8]

(ii) The second is to extend to tribal religion that attitude of sincere respect which we are trying to give to tribal life and institutions generally. No one should on any account criticise or laugh at any tribal ceremony or belief. Sometimes, the work of a well-trained higher officer may be completely undone by the ignorant folly of a clerk or a jawan. The same reverence should be shown by all members of our staff, should they be present at any tribal ceremony, that they would show in a Christian church or Hindu temple.[9]

(iii) As suggested in another chapter, we should be careful how we talk and about the words we use. Let us banish such expressions as 'superstition', 'heathen', 'devil dance' in relation to religion, just as we are trying to avoid generally such words as 'backward', 'uplift' and other patronizing expressions. We should not speak of 'animism' but we should speak of the 'Wancho religion' or the 'Adi religion', which will suggest that the tribal faith has for them just as much authority and dignity as the faith of the outside world. Care should be taken in

filling up any form, in which a person's religion is to be stated, that a tribesman should not be described as 'Hindu', 'Buddhist', 'Christian', unless he has formally adopted one of these religions or unless (as in parts of Kameng) one of the world religions, here, a Buddhism, has long since been accepted by the whole of tribe.[10]

(iv) Similarly, officers should use the local word for the Supreme Being whenever they have to speak of God; and oaths should be taken on the same name. Some simple prayer addressed in the local name of God might be composed, and in time our Research Department will, we hope, give us some collections of myths and legends and an account of the chief religions which can be translated and which will help to create that feeling of dignity and confidence in one's own culture, which is a secret of tribal vitality.[11]

II

MOVEMENT FOR RELIGIOUS IDENTITY

The process of forging of religious identity was initiated on 28th August 1968 when the Adi intellectuals held a meeting at Along, the district headquarters, to consider the means for forging a 'larger socio-religious association for forging a larger identity'.[12] It was decided to construct a Dony -Polo-Mopin-Solung-Dere' (Dony-Polo being the deity and divine figure of the Adis; Solung and Mopin being the most important festivals of Minyongs and Galos respectively, Dere being the community hall.'It "would provide a common meeting place for all communities" residing in the area on the occasion of "Social-cultural and religious celebrations such as Mopin and Solung" and "Generation for the Universal deity Donyi-Polo".[13] The 'germination' of the idea which "aimed at unification of Adi faith in the Supreme 'Donyi Polo' was welcomed by all".[14] The committee met on 13th March, 1969 and selected a suitable site within the township of Along. It was "decided to have an imposing structure made on in with religious and ritual motives of Adi religion so constructed that it would serve generation of Adi community and would be a monument to their rich hoary past.[15] The construction of the building was completed by the end of March, 1972.[16]

Search for religious identity has been the recurring theme in the writings of Adi intellectuals. In fact it has been the leitmotif of their ideology. In their perception religious identity and cultural identity are synonymous terms.[17] Thus forging of Donyipoloism as their religious identity has been the persistent effort with some of the intellectuals. The nomenclature Donyi-Polo religion, has been derived from the recognition of Donyi-Polo, the combined divine figure of Donyi (the Sun) and Polo (the moon), as Adis' popular gods.[18] According to Adi mythological accounts contained in the ballads called *abangs* by the Padam-Minyongs and *nyibo-agoms*, by the Galos, all beings and things of the universe have been created by the super-natural power or creator who is called Sedi by the Padam-Minyongs and Jimi by the Galos. It is Sedi who has created a number of gods and goddesses who in turn, gave birth to numerous invisible spirits who control the various spheres of the nature.[19] The narration in the *abangs* also says, "Sedi has a pair of searching eyes with which he keeps vigil on humanity. The two eyes are interpreted to be the Donyi (the Sun) and Polo (the moon).[20] "In the popular pantheon", says Nyori, "the name of Donyi-Polo (The Sun-Moon god) comes next to Sedi or Jimi, the creator. The creator becomes obscure and silent after the creation; so no sacrifice is offered to his name. On the other hand, the Adis give popular divine dignity to Donyi-Polo, the combined divine figure of Doni (the Sun) and Polo (the moon), which is regarded as the protector or Saviour."[21]

Basing on this tradition the intellectuals have been trying to construct religious identity called 'Donyi Poloism'. "Since people" according to Talom Rukbo "are ignorant of the philosophical basis of Donyi Poloism", they "embrace christianity and thus lose their own identity."[22] Therefore, he made it his mission of life to spread the meaning and philosophical basis of Donyi-Poloism. According to him 'Donyipolo' is almighty, omnipresent and omniscient.'[23] It governs the universe. It symbolises "truth, justice, morality, love and goodness."[24] The Adi intellectuals have constructed the belief systems, religious ethics and philosophy of Donyi Poloism, and published these in a booklet. These beliefs and principles were present in the day to day mundane existence of the people but these intellectuals have attributed abstract qualities to these beliefs and practices.[25] There is a detailed description of prayers which are and ought to be offered to Donyi Polo and which according to these intellectuals constitute Donyipolo faith and practice.[26] It is worthwhile to quote in full 'the concept, philosophy, and directive principles' of Donyi Poloism, as constructed by the intellectuals :

Concept

(1) It is the Universal truth and brotherhood.

(2) It is the supreme governing power of universe.

(3) It is ever probing power which is almighty, omnipresent, omnipotent and omniscient.

(4) It is the supreme judge of the highest court of law of eternal.

(5) It is the divine light, wisdom and knowledge.

(6) It is the source of life and energy of all living beings.

Philosophy

(1) All living and non-living beings are creation of Donyi-Polo.

(2) Purity, openness, frankness, truthfulness, love and peaceful co-existence are the eternal laws.

(3) Right, justice and kindness are path to the goal of Donyi-Polo.

(4) Equality, fraternity, self-respect and self-reliance are the qualities, qualification of Donyi-Polo faith.

(5) Mercy and apology with understanding are best solutions of any problem.

(6) Theft, hatred and lies are great sin.

Directive Principles

(1) Be frank and forward.

(2) Be prepared to help a helpless and according to capacity.

(3) Be prepared to adjust with any atmosphere and environment.

(4) Speak always truth.

(5) Love all as you love yourself.

(6) Treat all equal and brotherly.

(7) Respect elder and love to younger.

(8) Respect parents equal to god.

(9) Earn your bread with sweat and never depend on other.

(10) Don't laugh at crippled, deaf and blind lest it may repercus on you.

(11) Don't take anything beyond limit.

(12) Don't be ashamed to learn good things.

(13) Have faith on own culture and religion.

(14) Have regular prayer to Donyi Polo or God.

(15) Have courage to admit your own mistake.

(16) Have no fear to fight battle for truth and justice, Donyi-Polo helps you in such fight.

(17) Never back bite other.

(18) Never be tempted to what others have. Donyi-Polo provides you what you need.[27]

Then there is detailed description of prayers which are and ought to be offered to Donyi Polo and which according to the intellectuals constitute Donyi-Polo faith and practices.[28]

If we deconstruct these concepts, principles and the nature of the prayer we arrive at the conclusion that these intellectuals of the prayer we arrive at the conclusion that these intellectuals were motivated by the need to create normative principles for the younger generation. The ideas was to exercise hegemony over the minds of the rest of the society and lead the younger generation in the right direction.[29] There is a juxtaposition of precept to practice, of the organization of life as it should be, to the organization of life as it is. They have constructed an ideal image. They have given a theory of functioning which did not necessarily reflect the reality. The theory is the ideal image, worked out on the most careful classification of every detail. By creating a religious identity they have played a very significant role in : *(a)* preserving the values of society by recording the belief systems, religious ethics and philosophy of Donyi Polo faith and *(b)* bringing together through religious beliefs and practices various groups in the society. Culture thus becomes symbolic force in creating the unity in the society. The antidote to disintegrating forces of modernisation was a creation of organic culture coherent order of values capable of conferring a new meaning and unity in society.[30] It was to create a community bound together by shared norms and values.

III

Some of the intellectuals led by Talom Rukbo have further given more concrete form to Adi religion by establishing Donyi Polo Yelam Kebang (A Society of Donyi Polo Faith) in 1991. They have started "service of prayer on evening of every Saturday and mass gathering on every second Saturday for day service."[31] On 31st, December 1992, foundation of Donyi-Polo Altar building was laid along with raising of Donyi polo symbol.[32] Since then 31st, December is being celebrated as Donyi Polo day every year. Now-a-days every Saturday morning mass gathering takes places in Donyi Polo Gangin (temple) and mass prayer is performed accompanied by selected rituals.

In my filed survey in the Adi areas I observed it is largely women both in villages and in the urban areas, who attend the prayers on Saturdays. In the East Siang district and upper Siang this movement is spreading and it is observed that some of the persons who had embraced Christianity have also returned to their original faith and have started attending the prayers on Saturday.[33] But in Galo areas this movement has not yet become very popular.[34]

IV

But this form of mode of worship is being challenged by many intellectuals among the various sub-tribes of the Adis. Thus Oshong Ering one of the towering intellectuals belonging to Minyong group of the Adis and who has authored a large number of articles on Donyi-Poloism, explaining its philosophy etc., is not willing to accept this form of the movement. In his bio-data in the column 'Religion' (format provided by me) he wrote his religion as 'Natural'. Replying to my query, he said :

> I am hesistant to term Donyi Poloism as religion. But it is a tradition...Donyi-Polo does not simply mean Sun and Moon. If it would have been so they should have worshipped the Sun and Moon. But till today I have never seen the Adis worshipping the Sun and Moon. Only name is there. ...If tradition is called religion it may be so. But I am not sure about that...Traditionally Adis believe in Donyi-Polo but its actual ideological meaning is truth, peace, tranquility, wisdom, enlightenment. When you just sit in the *Kebang* when you talk abut truthfulness, when they say pray 'Donyi-Polo' ...not in God or anything of the sort... Donyi-Polo means truthfulness, enlightenment. ...They say Donyi. It is not God... I will speak only truth...Supreme light is the Donyi-Polo.[35]

Tumpak Ete, an intellectual belonging to Galo group of the Adis does not accept this form of religion as it has been shaped by Talom Rukbo. He argues that is an 'invention' an not an original religion.[36] 'Lot of innovation is there; and moreover, it is 'only confined to Pasighat area".[37]

But Talom Rukbo insists that this movement is not an invention and is only a 'reformation' basing entirely on the indigeneous traditions.[38] Kaling Borang another intellectual and associated with this movement, refutes the allegation of some that it is 'imitation' of Hinduism.[39] He does not rule out the 'influence' of outside religions but it does not 'indicate imitation'.[40] One may 'borrow' certain ideas from outside but 'once it is reworked and remodelled' that idea becomes 'our own'.[41] All the rituals and innovations, he argues 'are derived from our own indigeneous traditions."[42]

Thus the indigeneous intellectuals are not the passive rewarded recipients of the ideas imported from outside rather they have reworked, remodelled those ideas to suit their needs and have made these as an agenda of resistance against hegemony or played an active role in counter-hegemony or anti-hegemony. The forging of Dony Poloism, therefore, is an attempt at resistance to Christianity, Hinduism and all outside religions.

REFERENCES

1. A report of 1956-57, in Elwin Papers, File No. 110, p. 8.
2. K.L. Mehta's comments in a note dated 2-6-55 on some of the points arising on Dr. Elwin's note on a summary of experiences and Ideas gained during 1954-55, in Elwin Papers, File No. ATA/T/2, listed as File No. 133, p. 32.
3. *Ibid.*
4. *Ibid.*
5. In a confidential note Elwin stated that Shri Jairam Doulatram was the first to suggest that tribal religion should be developed. See Elwin Papers, File No. 153, p. 43.
6. Elwin papers, File No. ATA/T/2, listed as File No. 133, p. 32.
7. Verrier Elwin, B. Shastri and I. Simon, eds. *Important Directives on Administration of NEFA.* North-East Frontier Agency Administration, Shillong, 1967, p. 207. Emphasis added.
8. *Ibid.*, p. 207.
9. *Ibid.*, p. 207.
10. *Ibid.*, p. 208.
11. *Ibid.*, p. 208.
12. Donyi Polo Mopin Solung Dere, Along. The History of this event was inscribed on a stone pillar. Field Survey, 1988, February.
13. *Ibid.*

14. *Ibid.*
15. *Ibid.*
16. *Ibid.*
17. See Oshong Ering, 'Preservation and Revitalization of Cultural Heritage of Arunachal Pradesh", *Adi Cultural and Literary Society*, Pasighat, November 1976, pp. 5-11, Talom Rukbo, Foreword to *Donyi-Poloism* : Its *Faith and Practices*, Vol. i. Adi Cultural and Literary Society, Pasighat, September 1987. p. 1; T. Koyu, Preface to *Sedi-Melo Kelang among Telang A : Sang*, *Ibid.* p. iv; Tumpak Ete, Preface and Introduction, *Nyibu Agom* (The Sacred Lore of the Adis), Vol. i. pp. 1. 2, Date, Year and Place of Publication Not Mentioned; Talom Rukbo, Donyi-Poloism is a Concept, Not a Religion', *Echo*, November 23, 1980, p. 3 and 10th June 1987, p. 3. (This is Polemical Article Refuting Sanjay Takam's Allegation that Donyi-Polosim is not a Religion but a concept only. Sanjay Takam was Representing the Views of Catholics of Arunachal Pradesh and since then has emerged a very powerful, articulate and seasoned intellectual of Arunachal Pradesh and Now is a minister of cabinet rank in the present government. Talom Rukbo, 'Donyi-Poloism : A Religion not a Concept'. *Echo*, February 20, 1989, p. xiii; Talom Rukbo, 'Origin of Donyi-Polo Faith, *ibid*. August 15, 1989, pp. vii, x; Tamo Mibang. 'Indigeneous Faiths and Practices of The Minyongs", In Tanka B. Suba and Karubaki Datta, Eds. *Religion and Society in The Himalayas*, New Delhi, 1991, p. 140.
18. Oshong Ering, 'The Tanis and The Donyi-Polo Cult, *NEFA Information*, February 1970, pp. 22-25, Oshong Ering, 'Adi Belief and Faith', *Arunachal News*, Vol. 12, No. 5 August, 1983 pp. 25-26; Lummer Dai, 'Donyi-Polosim - A Scientific Religion', *Arunachal News*, Vol. 6, No. 4, 1977, pp. 56-58; Talom Rukbo, 'Donyi-Poloism : A Religion; *Arunachal Review*, July-December, 1985, pp. 1-4.
19. Oshong Ering, 'Religion of the Adis', *Arunachal News*, January 1980, pp. 31 - 34.
20. Tai Nyori, *History and Culture of the Adis*, New Delhi, 1993, p. 267.
21. *Ibid.*
22. Talom Rukbo, *Echo*, February 20, 1988, p. xiii
23. Talom Rukbo, *Echo*, February 28, 1988, p. 3.

24. Talom Rukbo, '*Donyi-Poloism : Its Faith and Practices,* Vol. i. p. 1; also see Oshong Ering, 'Preservation and Revitalization of Cultural Heritage of Arunachal Pradesh'. *Adi Cultural and Literary Society,* Pasighat, November 1976, p. 7.
25. *Dony-Poloism : Its Faith and Practices,* Vol. I. Published by Adi Cultural and Literary Society, Pasighat, September, 1987, pp. 1-16.
26. *Ibid.*
27. *Ibid.*, pp. 1-3.
28. *Ibid.*, pp. 3-16.
29. See Oshong Ering, *op. cit.*, P. 5.
30. For the concept of organic culture, See Raymond Williams, *Politics and Letters,* Interview with New Left Review, London, 1979, p. 114.
31. Talom Rukbo to The Secretary, Donyi-Polo Mission, Itanagar, October 23, 1991, in Talom Rukbo's Archive, File No. DPM (MC)/83-84.
32. Talom Rukbo to The Chairman, Donyi Polo Mission, Itanagar, Dated December 8, 1982 File No Acls-7/85-86. (Archives of Adi Cultural and Literary Society, Pasighat).
33. Field survey in Pasighat areas and Along areas in February 1998.
34. *Ibid.*
35. Personal Interview, Pasighat, February 15, 1998.
36. Personal Interview, Along February 23, 1998.
37. *Ibid.*
38. Personnel Interview, Pasighat, February 15, 1998.
39. Personnel Interview, Pasighat, February 21, 1998.
40. *Ibid.*
41. *Ibid.*
42. *Ibid.*

Chapter - 7
Medium of Instruction, Tribal Languages and Identity

I
OFFICIAL DISCOURSE

The policy-makers were convinced that the knowledge of the tribal language was an essential prerequisite for creating legitimacy in NEFA :

> A knowledge of the language is the window by which we see into the tribal mind; it is the door through which we shall most readily receive tribal affection and cooperation... it is also the most prerequisite of achieving our ideal of identifying ourselves with the tribal people.[1]

Therefore, it was decided to 'develop' and 'strengthen' the tribal languages.[2] It was made obligatory on the part of the officials as well as school teachers to learn the tribal dialects.[3] 'Substantial rewards' were proposed to be offered to the officers for "preparing grammars, primers, dictionaries etc."[4] It was resolved to introduce respective mother-tongues at the primary level education[5] and the script for these languages was proposed to be Devanagari.[6] Language officers were appointed to prepare text books and supplementary reading materials.[7] Students were encouraged to write stories, features and articles in their mother-tongues, for school magazines.[8]

I (b)

ENCOURAGEMENT TO HINDI LANGUAGE

The introduction of Hindi language in NEFA formed another aspect of this official discourse of exercising nationalist hegemony.[9] Hindi was sought to provide "some kind of cultural link between NEFA and the rest of the country."[10] It was desired to have " a Hindi-speaking NEFA."[11] A policy document's seventh chapter devoted to the question of language, states :

> Hindi is the national language and it was so established by the great architects of our country's freedom to be a primary instrument of unity between rich and poor, learned and illiterate, plainsman and hillman, as well as between the varied multi-lingual people of India.
>
> It has been now decided that Hindi will become the medium of higher instruction in NEFA and, in time, the lingua franca that will unite not only the diverse populations within its borders but also its people with the people of the plains, who themselves as loyal citizens will naturally be also learning the same language.
>
> All our officers, therefore, should not only learn Hindi themselves, but also should encourage its study in every way among the tribal people in their care.[12]

II

MIDDLE CLASS IN ASSAM AND ITS ATTITUDE TO HINDI

The inclination towards Hindi aroused strong antagonism in Assam. The various members of the civil society in Assam had been asserting that the relationship between NEFA and Assam 'is natural and inseparable from the point of history and geography',[13] and therefore "NEFA should be merged with Assam as provided by the Constitution."[14] In the aftermath of Indo-China war of 1962 the movement for merger of NEFA with Assam was intensified in Assam. Thus representatives of different College Unions of Gauhati met on April 6, 1963 under the Presidentship of Shri Prafulla Barua, President of the Gauhati Inter College Defence Union, and decided to form the NEFA-Assam integration Student's Committee with the aim of taking "necessary steps for the emotional integration between NEFA and Assam."[15] Shri Ratnakanta Barkakati, eminent poet of Assam, in his Presidential address to the 30th session of Assam Sahitya Sabha held at Nazira from April 19 to April 21, 1963 "passionately appealed for the rapid integration of NEFA with Assam" and advocated the idea of spreading Assamese language and adoption of Assamese script for the languages of the hill areas.[16] Presiding over the 31st session of the Assam Sahitya Sabha at Digboi on April 18, 1964, Shri Mitradev Mahanta said that the fact that NEFA was administered by the central Government and most of the officers in NEFA happened to be non-Assamese did not warrant that the language in the area should be non-Assamese. He strongly pleaded for introduction of Assamese language in NEFA.[17] Simultaneously, the General Secretary, Dr. Maheswar Neog gave a trenchant criticism of language policy in education of the NEFA administration.[18]

In an article in *The Assam Tribune* for June 12, 1956 titled 'Assamese in NEFA' the author stated "For ages past as a result of many-sided contact, Assamese has been enjoying the position of a lingua-franca among the tribals of the region."[19] he further remarked that the teaching of the national language (Hindi) will drive the tribals further apart from their brethren in the plains by superimposing cultural segregation on political segregation.[20]

In the face of such criticism the NEFA administration decided to introduce changes in 1959.

Leo L. Rose and Margaret W. Fisher write :

> It was decided that local NEFA languages should henceforth be written in the Assamese scripts rather than the devanagari...The medium of instruction at the lower level was still to be the local language, but at the middle and higher levels, where possible, it was to be Assamese. The teaching of Assamese at the primary level was retained as a compulsory subject, but Hindi (which previously had been compulsory also) was to be made an additional subject only.[21]

III

RESISTANCE AGAINST HINDI AND ASSEMESE : ANTI-HEGEMONY

The hegemonistic tendencies of both Hindi as well Assamese were contested by the intellectuals of NEFA Arunachal Pradesh. In a representation dated September 1, 1959 to the Advisor to the Governor of Assam, Shillong, the NEFA college students from Shillong resisted against both the Assamese as well as Hindi hegemony on the question of medium of instruction and script for the tribal languages. Speaking on behalf of the people of NEFA and Adis in particular, they wrote :

> no one of them (Adis and the people of NEFA) is willing to accept Assamese medium and Assamese script for NEFA or Siang Frontier Division. But non-acceptance of Assamese medium and Assamese script does not mean that they (we) are prepared to welcome Hindi medium and Davanagari script.[22]

In another representation by Takam Kana from NEFA hostel, Shillong, dated June 12, 1962 to the Commissioner, North-East Frontier Agency, Shillong, it was asserted that "the outsiders whether they are Assamese speaking or Hindi-speaking people have no right and authority to interfere" on the question of medium of instruction and demanding for medium of their languages in NEFA schools.[23] It raised the question of indigeneous people's right for self-determination on the question of language.[24] The author also took up the issue of 'emotional integration'. When the Assamese language could not bring about unity of different ethnic groups inhabiting Assam, then, how is it expected to perform the task of 'emotional integration' of NEFA with Assam', and 'NEFA with Delhi'? The author avered.[25] On the other hand, imposition of Assamese language in NEFA would generate anti-Assamese sentiments.[26]

The intellectuals suggested adoption of alternative script for the tribal languages. While Khamptis of Lohit Frontier Division and the Monpas of Kameng Frontier Division had their own indigeneous scripts, the other tribes did not have their own indigeneous scripts. The Khamptis and Monpas had started reviving their original scripts. The intellectuals of the Aids of the Siang Frontier Division preferred to adopt Roman script for their languages. While advocating the justifiability of adoption of Roman script, the Adi intellectuals pointed out "The Roman script had already been adopted in the beginning of 20th century" by Christian Missionaries.[27] They had translated Bible in Adi languages in the Roman Script.[28] Quite a number of Adis, "both villagers and students know how to read and write in this script."[29] Moreover, the Roman Script was perceived to be "phonetic, scientific and fit for the language of Adis."[30] They asserted that Roman script is easier than either the Devanagari or Assamese script.[31]

The intellectuals in NEFA demanded English as the medium of instruction besides developing their mother tongues.[32] There was no objection to the introduction of Hindi as a compulsory language because it was felt that being the national language, it would facilitate the NEFA people to visit the different places in India without any communication problem.[33] Therefore, the students of NEFA launched a movement for introduction of English as the medium of instruction during 1960's.[34]

IV

RESISTANCE TO THE INTRODUCTION OF SANSKRIT

Some of the intellectuals from Arunachal also resisted the move by the State Government to introduce Sanskrit as a third language in the Schools of Arunachal Pradesh in 1991. In a petition dated April 5, 1991 signed by twenty-seven post-graduate students and Research scholars from Aruanchal Pradesh Registered in Delhi University and Jawaharlal Nehru University, New Delhi wrote to the Chief Minister :

> That Sir, this proposed step of the Government has come in the midst of our growing fear over the undue prominence being given to Hindi in the state, which has even made the tribal people to discard their own dialects in favour of it (Hindi). Though we do not have anything against the learning of Hindi

> as such, but when it goes to the extent of undermining and eroding our very own dialects, we feel that it is a matter of serious concern for all of us.[35]

They asserted that :

> the present step to introduce Sanskrit in the state will further accelerate this process and cause immense and irreversible damage to the rich dialects that we have inherited.[36]

The opponents of Sanskrit were denounced by the *Echo*,[37] a weekly newspaper from Arunachal Pradesh in its issue of April 17/24 :

> There are some forces who are trying to clean away people from this language by misguiding and inciting others. ...The people also should guard themselves against being influenced by these divisive forces.[38]

In turn, it invited scathing criticism form one Tony Pertin. In a letter dated May 29, 1991 to The Acting -Editor, *Echo* he alleged that this newspaper is biased towards Hindi and Hinduism and is anti-Christian.[39] This letter provides a critique of the article titled 'Sanskrit – the binding force for one's unity and culture' published in the *Echo* of 17/24 of April, 1991. He retorted :

> People who are known for dirty practices like casteism, bride-burning etc. has no moral right or business interfering in our culture and give sermons to the people as to what language they should learn and what religion they should follow. Arunachal people are mature enough and let them decide the matter for themselves.[40]

He questioned the view that Sanskrit is the binding force for one's unity and culture. He wrote :

> If you think that any particular culture is the culture of the nation as a whole, simply because it is followed by the majority or because it being the oldest, and thus everybody, including the ethnic and cultural minorities must accept it, it is a blatant attempt to impose the cultural hegemony of the majority on the minority. Any unity that is achieved by destroying the diversity, as was done by Fascists in the first half of the century, is not a real unity and will not last long. Any meaningful unity

> must be achieved by first recognising and respecting the cultural diversity of the people. Your view on unity and integration is, thus, the same as that of the R. S. S.[41]

He warns :

> Any arrogant and forceful imposition of an outside language on the people against their will, in the name of unity and national integration, could prove counter-productive in the long run. It might succeed today, but at certain stage when people become conscious and suddenly discover that their culture and identity have been diluted in the process of national integration, they will lose faith and develop hatred for the nation and the process of national integration. Thus, the main goal of unity and integration which you propose to generate through the promotion of Sankskrit will not only become meaningless but also could prove counterproductive.[42]

V

INDIGENEOUS INTELLECTUALS AND THE DEVELOPMENT OF TRIBAL LANGUAGES

The movement for developing the tribal languages in NEFA was generated by the creation of various public spheres or public spaces, especially the cultural and literary societies. The Adis and Khamptis were the first to form such organizations. 'The Adi Cultural and Literary Society' was formally inaugurated at Along, the district headquarters, 'with a two-day programme on 14th and 15th November, 1971.[43] Since then a large number of societies have been formed and registered in different parts of Arunachal Pradesh.[44] These Associations have been the arenas of forging of cultural identities of the respective tribes and the development of their languages forms an important aspect of this agenda.

Besides, these Associations, various other forums (Public spaces) have also been established. Thus in the Adi areas, the various public spaces formed were : Adi Cultural and Literary Society, Pasighat; Bogum Bokang Kebang, Pasighat; Adi cultural and Literary society, Roing; Adi Agom Kebang (Adi Sahiya Sabha), Pasighat; Eastern Adi Students Union, East Siang District, Pasighat; Eastern Siang Students, Union, Pasighat etc.

The forging of cultural identity by a social group generally involves the process of homegenisation of various aspects of culture, and the creation of a common language forms an important aspect of this process. In other words, the identity is not something given, it is constructed, it is a part of the cultural politics. Thus among the Adis this process of evolving a common language goes back to 1950's. The Adis, linguistically belong to a larger group called Tani group of tribes. These are: Nishing, Tagins, Apatanis, Hill Miris and Misings of the Brahmaputra valley.[45] In 1959, Shri Oshong Ering suggested to the Adviser to the Governor of Assam that "people of these tribes, inspite of their dialectical variation, speak the same 'Tani Agom' or 'Human language'. He stated :

> Among them, they talk to one another in their dialects and they understand each other. This shows that these people can have a Written Language in course of time. This can be possible if the *Authority* encourages them to do so from now on.[46]

Therefore, he suggested the "possibility of fostering a prosperous 'Tani Agom' or 'Human Language' for the aforesaid tribes." He demanded the state patronage for production of text books keeping this in view.[47]

But it remained just a suggestion and no concrete step has ever been taken to develop a common language of all the tribes of Tani group. However, a sustained attempt had been taken to evolve a common Adi language and has been still going on. The attempt to create a common language for all the Adi groups of tribes can be traced back to 1950's. The NEFA administration had taken steps to produce Text Books basing the language spoken at Pasighat area.[48] In the meeting of the Adi Language Committee held at Pasighat on 22nd March, 1958 "all the members present agreed that there should be one common language for the entire Siang Frontier Division."[49] It was agreed that "the present Text Books written by the Administration in the language spoken at present in the Pasighat area should be accepted immediately to serve as the foundation and skeleton for all future books for the Division."[50] However, a member belonging to Galo group Shri Tajum Koyu was "hesitant to accept this opinion" without consulting other members of the Galos. The meeting continued on March 23, 1958 and Shri Tamo Riba, Tapak Ringu and other senior students of the local H. E. School were invited to offer their views. The opinion of the members was divided as on the previous day. Some of the senior students particularly of the Galong group opposed the immediate introduction of the text books in the schools.[51]

In fact the opposition to the Adi text books was very strong in the Galong areas. It was alleged by the Galong intellectuals that this is Minyong – Padam-pasi language and Galo words and symbols have not been included.[52] At Along the opposition was so strong that a group led by Bokan Ete as Talom Rukbo reminiscences "collected all Adi books and burnt."[53] Therefore, the administration withdrew these books from the Gallong areas.[54]

The Gallong intellectuals' opposition to the Adi text books has been expressed from item to time. Thus in a letter to The President, Adi Agom Kebang dated February 12, 1984 three intellectuals Shri Eto Ete, Shri Kali Ngulom, Shri Jumte Kadu wrote :

> The intellectuals membership presented in Your 'Adi Agom Kebang' appears to be one sided, as several community of 'Adi' are not represented fully. The policies and words adoptd are originally from 'Padam', Minyong', and 'Pasi' which has created confusion in the conscious of the 'Adi' community like 'Galo', 'Bori', 'Bokar' etc.[55]

Recently, some of the intellectuals among Gallong have been campaigning for asserting a separate identity for the Galos. A meeting of cross section of Galos of Arunachal Pradesh residing at the capital complex was held at Siddharth Hall on June 10, 1999 under the chairmanship of Shri Takap Ringu.[56] Addressing the meeting, Shri Horsen Ete, the Chief convenor said :

> Whereas the Constitution (Scheduled Tribes) order 1950 in 3rd. Schedule recognises Galong as a major Tribe of Arunachal Pradesh, the Galong Tribe has nowhere been made a sub-tribe

or subservient to ADI (Abor) Tribe anywhere in any of the constitutional amendments made so far and whereas Government has been issuing Schedule Tribe certificates to Galo in the name of ADI with Galong bracketed which signifies Galong as a sub-tribe of ADI unlike Minyong, Padam etc.[57]

He further stated that "there is an imperative need to redefine the boundaries so that no vested interest exploit the Galos in the name of unity of the ADI tribe which has now been a misnomer for the Galos."[58]

To take the final decision in this regard 'Galo Bogum-Bokang Kebang' was held at Alo (Along) on January 10-11, 2000 whereas about five to six thousand Galos gathered and debated on this question.[59] It was resolved to maintain a separate identity of the Galos as per the Constitution. A Galo Welfare Society was formed and development of Galo language was meant to be one of its aims.[60] However, a group of intellectuals among the Galos have asserted themselves to retain the former Adi identity and they have been campaigning for this purpose.[61] An 'Extra Ordinary Bogum Bokang Conference' (of all the Adi groups) was held on August 19-20, 2000 at Naharlagun (Itanagar) to discuss this question. I, myself attended the conference both these days and took the detailed notes of this conference. Some of the Galo intellectuals favoured retention of the Adi identity and some others advocated a separate identity. However, finally it was resolved to retain not only the Adi identity but lead a movement for strengthening the Adi identity. But still many intellectuals of the Galo group have not accepted the verdict of this resolution and are campaigning for a separate identity.

To conclude this chapter : identity is not something fixed forever but is a product of history. It is a process and goes on evolving. It is a construct and is negotiable.

REFERENCES

1. D. O. Letter No. 56/55 dated October 21, 1955 in Elwin Papers, File No. 166 (listed), p. 51.
2. *Ibid.*

3. File No. ATA/G/62, listed as File No. 101, p. 46. (Elwin papers).
4. 'Summary of proceedings of Hill officers Conference held at Shillong from April 10, 1953 to April 15th 1953, in Elwin Papers, File No. ATA/P/2, listed as File No. 111, p. 9.
5. A talk by Shri K. L. Mehta, I.C.S. From All India Radio, Shillong, On September 1, 1955, in Elwin Papers, File No. 149 (Listed), p. 28; Also See File No. 166, p. 52; Also see Supplementary Note in File No. Ed 3/13/62 Dated April 1962, from Deputy Commissioner (A) North-East Frontier Agency, Shillong to the Under-Secretary to the Government of India, Ministry of External Affairs, New Delhi, in Talom Tukbo's Personnel Archive.
6. *Ibid.*
7. The Deputy Commissioner (A) North-East Frontier Agency, Shillong to the Under-Secretary to the Government of India, Ministry of External Affairs, New Delhi, No. Ed/13/62 April 1962, Starred Parliament Question 2451 For Second May. In Talom Rukbo's Personnel Archive File No. PF/68/, p. 35.
8. *Ibid.*
9. T. N. Kaul to K. L. Mehta, Adviser to the Governor of Assam, April 10, 1956, Confidential letter No. 2701, JS (E) in Elwin Papers, File No. ATA/T/2 listed as File No. 133.
10. See Shri B. Keskar, Minister of Information and Broadcasting, India. Confidential letter No. 34-S/61-M.O. dated New Delhi, February 1961 to Nehru Prime Minister, New Delhi.
11. A note by The Financial Adviser, Shri. R. M. Aggarwal in a confidential note by Verrier Elwin in Elwin Papers, File No. 153, p. 44.
12. Elwin Papers, File No. 166, pp. 52-53; also see File No. 151 (listed), p. 27.
13. Confidential note of the President Assam Pradesh Congress Committee to the Members of the Assam Pradesh Congress executive Committee, point. No. 10, 23-7-53, in *Proceedings of the Assam Pradesh Congress Executive Committee Meeting*, Microfilm in Nehru Memorial Library and Centre for Contemporary Studies, Teen Murti House, New Delhi.
14. Resolution of the Joint 'Meeting of the Assam Pradesh Congress Executive Committee and the Assam Congress Parliamentary Party Executive Meeting held at Congress

Bhavan, Gauhati on April 26, 1955 to 27 April 1955 in *Proceedings of the Assam Pradesh Congress Executive Committee, op. cit.*

15. *Assam Tribune,* April 19, 1963, p. 3.
16. *Ibid.*, April 21, 1963, p. 6.
17. *Ibid.*, April 19, 1964, p. 1.
18. *Ibid.*, April 20, 1964, p. 2.
19. Notes on the leading article in *Assam Tribune,* June 12, 1956 entitled 'Assamese in NEFA' in Elwin Papers, File No. ATA/ c/7 (listed as File No. 31).
20. Cited in *ibid.*
21. Leo E. Rose and Margaret M. Fisher, *op. cit.*, p. 44.
22. NEFA College Students, Shillong to the Adviser to the Governor of Assam, Shillong, September 1, 1959. In Talom Rukbo's personnel Archive. This representation was signed by sixteen (16) students of undergraduate classes and all of them belonged to Adi group of tribes.
23. Talom Rukbo's Archives.
24. *Ibid.*
25. *Ibid.*
26. *Ibid.*
27. See representation by NEFA College Students, Shillong to the Adviser to the Governor of Assam, Shillong, dated September 1, 1959 in Talom Rukbo's Archive; also see Resolution No. 3 passed by the Bogum Bokang Kebang held at Balek on June 2, 1962 in Secretary, Bogum Bokang Kebang to the Commissioner, NEFA, Shillong, June 15, 1962 in Talom Rukbo's Archive.
28. *Ibid.*
29. *Ibid.*
30. Secretary, Bogum Bokang Kebang to the Commissioner Shillong, June 15, 1962, In Talom Rukbo's Archive.
31. *Ibid.*
32. *Ibid.*

33. *Ibid.*; Also Interview with Oshong Ering, Pasighat, February 15, 1998.
34. Interview with Shri Hitum Loya, Head Gam Pauk Ghat, Along, Dated February 25, 1998.
35. Talom Rukbo's personal Archive.
36. *Ibid.*
37. Cited in Tony Pertin's Letter dated May 1991 to Talom Rukbo and a copy to the Acting-Editor, *Echo* of Arunachal, Itanagar. Tony Pertin, a Student of LLB, Delhi University Wrote this letter on Behalf of many other students studying in Delhi University and Jawaharlal Nehru University, The address given is 107, Mansarovar Hostel, University of Delhi-110007.
38. *Ibid.*
39. *Ibid.*
40. *Ibid.*
41. *Ibid.*
42. *Ibid.*
43. See Jayanta Kumar Sarkar, 'Development of identity Consciousness in Arunachal Pradesh', *op. cit.*, pp. 231-40.
44. *Op., cit.*
45. Tai Nyori, *op.cit.*, p.4.
46. Oshong Ering to the Adviser to the Governor of Assam, Shillong, September 7, 1959, in Talom Rukbo's Archive, File No. PF/68, p. 10.
47. *Ibid.*
48. Interview with Oshong Ering, Pasighat, dated February 15, 1998.
49. Proceedings of the Meeting of the Adi Language Committee Held at Pasighat on 22nd March 1958 drafted by R. K. Patri and a copy forwarded to Talom Rukbo. In Talom Rukbo's personal Archives.
50. *Ibid.*
51. *Ibid.*
52. Interview with Tumpak Ete, Along dated February 23, 1998, Marjum Loyi, Along, February 25, 1998.

53. Interview with Talom Rukbo, Pasighat, dated February 22, 1998; also see interview with Oshong Ering, Pasighat, dated February 15, 1998.
54. Talom Rukbo, *ibid.*
55. File No. Nil. Office of Adi Cultural and Literary Society, Pasighat.
56. Minutes of the Meeting Held on January 10, 1999, of the Galos, in T. Riba's collection.
57. *Ibid.*
58. *Ibid.*
59. Interview with Tomo Riba, Arunachal University campus, Rono Hills, dated April 13, 2000.
60. *Ibid.*
61. *Ibid.*

Chapter - 8
Concluding Remarks without Conclusions

The official discourse of 'integration' of NEFA with the Indian nationalist 'mainstream' was that of exercising of cultural hegemony. It had two aspects *(a)* appropriation of tribal cultural practices and *(b)* introduction of 'mainstream' culture. Though the first predominated during the period 1950 to 1964 and the second in the post Indo-China war period *i.e.* after 1962 (specifically after 1964 after Elwin and Nehru's death) but the strains of the 'mainstream' cultural hegemony were felt during the 1950's too, simultaneously. The cultural movement, especially the movement for cultural identity among the Adis of Arunachal Pradesh evolved out of the dialogue with this official discourse. The intellectuals among the Adi tribe who were actively engaged in this dialogue with the official discourse partially appropriated this discourse too. But in the process of appropriation they evolved their own agenda of resistance against the officially sponsored 'cultural hegemony' and carved out their own space of forging a process of identity formation.

This process of identity formation expressed itself in various ways. Firstly, it gushed out in a violent form against the outside religious symbols, especially against Christianity and secondly, it demanded state protection of their religious beliefs and practices *vis-a-vis* outside religious propaganda. The result was the passage of 'Arunachal Pradesh Freedom of

Indigeneous Faith 1978 Bill' passed by the Arunachal Legislative Assembly which was given assent by the President of India, with certain modifications and it came to be known as 'The Arunachal Pradesh Freedom of Religion Act, 1978 (Act No. 4 of 1978).

Thirdly, the intellectuals started taking resort to defence of their cultural practices and the formation of Adi Cultural and Literary Society and some other forums was an important aspect of this agenda for cultural defence. The most important aims and objectives of these societies have been the preservation of traditional cultural heritage. The tradition, however, was not perceived by them as something fixed and permanent but dynamic one. And therefore, it also involved the process of modification, reformation of some of the popular cultural practices which were being perceived as hindrance towards progress of the society. These were : bride-price, child-marriage, forced-marriage sacrifice of animals etc. Whatever was suitable for the existing needs of the society, was selected and appropriated by the intellectuals and then passed on as tradition. In other words, the tradition got reformulated in favour of the emerging educated class.

However, the forging of cultural identity also involved the question of women. It were the male intellectuals who first of all took up the women's questions. But, gradually, when the percentage of educated women had increased in the Siang frontier division, it was realised by women intellectuals that women's problems have to be confronted by women themselves and therefore they started organising themselves and the result was the formation of Arunachal Women's Welfare Society, Itanagar on October 10, 1979. The Adi Women intellectuals, too, established its branch in Along, simultaneously.

Another aspect of the movement for cultural identity among the Adis has been the movement for religious identity. It has been a recurring theme in the writings of the Adi intellectuals. They have constructed the belief systems, religious ethics and philosophy of this religion based on tribal traditions, it has been called by them as 'Donyipoloism'. However, some of the intellectuals have provided a concrete form to this religious identity by establishing 'Donyi Polo Yelam Kebang' (A society of Donyipolo Faith). They have established temples and it has been developing in some of the Adi areas but some of the intellectuals have contested this form of religious identity and the movement is moving forward inspite of hostility to it by some of the Adi educated persons.

The development of tribal languages had been an important aspect of the movement for cultural identity in Arunachal Pradesh. However, the discourse for developing the tribal languages had to contend itself against the hegemony of Assamese, Hindi and Sanskrit languages and out of this contestation emerged an effort to evolve a common language on the part of the Adi intellectuals. However, the process of homogenisation of the Adi language got contested by intellectuals of the Galo group of the Adis. Their assertion was that this proposed homogeneous language to be evolved out of the amalgamation of diverse dialects spoken by various sub-tribes of the Adis did not take into account the dialect spoken by the Galos. They argued that this language was based on the dialect spoken in the Pasighat areas. Therefore, they resisted against this move and ultimately culminated into the process of demanding a separate identity on the part of some of the intellectuals of Galo group of the Adis. But this separate identity on the part of some of the Galo intellectuals got contested by another group of Galo intellectuals who are in favour of retaining the common Adi identity. This process of identity formation (a separate one on the part of Galos and its contestation by others) is going on and that is why we have put the title of this chapter as 'concluding remarks without conclusion'. Only the future generation of Galos and other groups of the Adis would decide whether to retain the Adi identity or forge their separate independent autonomous identities.

APPENDIX – A

Interviews Conducted

I had conducted large number of interviews in the course of my field work but here a list of the most prominent intellectuals is being provided with whom I had long spell of conversations. No structured type of interviews were conducted. Some basic questions were asked to initiate the discussion and the rest of questions evolved out of the conversation itself. However the entire conversation was recorded with the help of tape-recorder.

The following names are being listed here :

1. Talom Rukbo.
2. Oshong Ering.
3. Lummer Dai.
4. Tumpak Ete.
5. Dagmo Jini.
6. Tagang Taki.
7. Hitum Loya.
8. Smt. Hitum Loya.
9. Mrs. Jarjum Ete.
10. Mis Hoksum Eshi.
11. Prof. Tamo Mibang.
12. Dr. Tai Nyori.
13. Dr. Tomo Riba.
14. Shri Tomi Ete.
15. Shri Marjum Loyi.

Appendix – B

The following format for conducting interview was used to derive the basic information. The signature of the person interviewed was taken after having got the form filled, and permission of the person was taken to quote him in the report.

FORMAT

1. Date
2. Time
3. Name
4. Date of Birth
5. Age
6. Gender
7. Father's Name
8. Mother's Name
9. Tribe
10. Sub-tribe
11. Clan
12. Religion
13. District
14. Police Station
15. Village
16. Educational Qualification - with details from school level to the University level
17. Profession
18. Member of any Literary and Cultural Society
19. Member of any Political Party
20. Marital Status
21. Signature

Appendix – C

Sample of the Questions

The following is the sample of some of the questions asked to initiate the conversation.

1. Narrate your life history from your childhood to the present.
2. What were the influences upon you?
3. Which type of books you used to read and why?
4. What made you to think of social problems?
5. Why did you start this Association?
6. What made you write on your cultural and religious affairs?
7. Why are you against outside religions?
8. Why are you against Christianity?
9. What do you think of the various welfare programmes introduced by Christian missionaries?
10. Narrate the history of Christianity in your area?
11. What made you start this type of movement, that is the movement against christianity?
12. Why did you develop your religion in this form?
13. Did you follow or borrow from other religious organisations to develop your religion?
14. What made you develop your tribal language?
15. Should there be a common Adi language?
16. What do you think of Women's problems?
17. Why women intellectuals are taking up women's questions?
18. What do you think of women's movement in other parts of India?
19. What are your future plans?

Bibliography

(A)

Field Data

I took extensive field work in December 1997, January 1998 and February 1998. In the month of February 1998. I visited Pasighat, Along, Bolang, Basar and Pangin towns and surrounding villages. Large number of interviews were taken. And on the Basis of these interviews some of the generalisations in this report have been used.

(B)

Official Records, Reports, Private Papers Etc.
Both Published and Unpublished

1. Census Reports, 1971, 1981 and 1991.
2. *Official Report*, Proceedings of the Arunachal Pradesh First Legislative Assembly, second session, 17, 18 and 19th May, 1978. Assembly Secretariat, Arunachal Pradesh, Naharlagun (Itanagar).
3. *The Arunachal Pradesh Code*, volume iii, Acts made by the Arunachal Pradesh Legislative Assembly, Government of Arunachal Pradesh Law and Judicial Department, Itanagar, 1982.
4. Verrier Elwin, B. Shastri and I. Simon, eds., *Important Directives on Administration of NEFA*, North-East Frontier Agency Administration, Shillong, 1967.
5. *Techno-Economic Survey of NEFA*, National Council of Applied Economic Research, New Delhi, December 1967.

6. Elwin Papers, Private Papers of Verrier Elwin, Manuscript Section of Nehru Memorial Museum and Library and Centre for Contemporary Studies, Teen Murti House, New Delhi.

I consulted Elwin papers related to the period 1953 to 1964 during which period he had been appointed as the Adviser, Tribal Affairs to the Governor of Assam.

7. Jairam Das Doulat Ram papers, *ibid.*

8. Gopinath Bordoloi's Papers, *ibid.*

(C)

Other Records : N.G.O's, Newspapers, and Writings of Intellectuals

1. All the files and other records maintained by Adi cultural and literary society, Pasighat since its very inception.
2. By-Laws and Constitution of Arunachal Pradesh Women's Welfare Society.
3. Records maintained by Arunachal Pradesh Women's Welfare Society, Along.
4. Proceedings of the Assam Pradesh Congress Working Committee, Microfilm, Nehru Memorial Museum and Library, Teen Murti House, New Delhi.
5. Ering, Oshong, *Donyi-Polo- Faith and belief of The Tani.* Donyi-Polo Mission, Itanagar, Series - 1.
6. Koyu, T., *Sedi-Melo Kelang Among Telang Abang.*
7. Rukbo, Talom, *Donyi-Poloism : Its faith and Practices.*
8. *Nyibu Agom* : By Tumpak Ete.
9. *Bogum Bokang Kebang*, 19-20th August 2000, Nahar Lagun, Itanagar.
10. Personnel Archives maintained by Talom Rukbo.
11. T. Riba's collection.

12. *Arshi* (Mirror) a journal published by Adi Cultural and Literary Society, Pasighat.
13. All the Poems written by the Talom Rukbo.
14. All the Poems written by Prof. T. Mibang, his personnel collection.
15. All the Novels published (authored by) Lummer Dai.
16. *Echo*, newspaper (first weekly, then bi-weekly and daily) from Itanagar.
17. *Arunachal News*, Itanagar.
18. *NEFA Information*, February 1970.
19. *Assam Tribune*, 1950 to 1980. District Library, Guwahati, Assam.
20. *Arunachal Times*, Naharlagun.
21. The Hindu September 18, 1978.
22. *National Council of Christian Review*, 1980 to 1990. Headquarters of Norht-East Council of Baptist Christian Association, Pan Bazar, Guwahati.

Articles Cited

1. Althusser, Louis, 'Ideology and Idelogical State Apparatus' in Louis Althusser, *Lenin and Philosophy*, Trans, Ben Brewester (New Left Books, 1971).
2. Bordoloi, B.N., 'Administration of Tribal Areas *vis-a-vis* the Sixth Schedule to the Constitution of India-the Founding Fathers' views', Vivekananda Patrika, (date and issue not mentioned).
3. Bourdieu, Pierre, 'The aristocracy of culture', *Media, Culture, Society*, Vol. 2, No. 3, 1980.
4. Bhattacharya, Sabyasachi, 'Notes on the role of the intelligentsia in Colonial Society : India from mid nineteenth century', *Studies in History*, Vol. 1, Number 1, January-June 1979.
5. Chartier, Roger, 'Culture as Appropriation : Popular Cultural Uses in Early Modern France', in Kaplan,

Steven. L. ed. *understanding Popular Culture* : **Europe** *from the Middle Ages to the Nineteenth Century,* Berlin, Mouton Publishers, 1984.

6. Chakravarty, Dipesh, 'of Garbage, Modernity and the citizen's Gaze', *Economic and Political Weekly,* March 7-14, 1993.
7. Chatterjee, Partha "Talking about our Modernity in Two Languages', in Partha Chatterjee, (*A Possible India,* Essays in Political Criticism, (Delhi : Oxford University Press, 1997).
8. Dawar, Jagdish Lal, 'Nationalist Hegemony and Popular Culture in Arunachal Pradesh : A case study of responses to video-Cinema in Doimukh Circle of Papum-pare District', *Proceedings of North-East India History Association,* Agartala, 1997.
9. Dai, Lummer, 'Donyi-Poloism – Scientific Religion', *Arunachal News,* Vol. 6, No. 4, 1977, pp. 56-58.
10. Dyer, Richard, 'Entertainment and Utopia' in During, Simon, ed. *The Cultural Studies Reader,* Routledge, London, 1993.
11. Dawar, Jagdish Lal, 'Movement for Cultural Identity since 1950 among the Mishmis of Arunachal Pradesh', *Proceedings of North-East India History Association,* Silchar, 1995.
12. Ering, Oshong, 'Child-marriage in Adi Society and Plight of Girls', *Arunachal News,* August 1981, pp. 9-12.
13. ...'The Tanis and the Donyi-Polo Cult, *NEFA Information,* February 1970, pp. 22-25.
14. ...'Adi belief and faith', *Arunachal News,* Vol. 12, No. 5. August 1983, pp. 25-26.
15. ...'Religion of the Adis '*Arunachal News,* January 1980, pp. 31-34.
16. Hobsbawm, Eric, 'Introduction : Invention of Tradition' in Hobsbawm, Eric and Terence Ranger,

The Invention of Tradition, Cambridge University Press, Cambridge, 1983.

17. Inden, Ronald, 'Transnational Class, Erotic Arcadia and Commercial Utopia in Hindi films' in Christiane Brosius and Melissa Butcher, eds., *Image Journey* : Audio-Visual Media and Cultural Change in India, Sage Publication, New Delhi, Thousand Oaks, London, 1999.
18. Jameson, Fredric, 'Reification and Utopia in Mass Culture', in Jameson, Fredric, *Signature of Visible*, Durham, 1989.
19. Kesing, Roger M., 'Theories of Culture', *Annual Review of Anthropology*, Vol. 3, 1974, pp. 73-97.
20. Lear, Jackson T. J., 'The Concept of Cultural Hegemony : Problems and Possibilities', *The American Historical Review*, Vol. 90, No. 3, June, 1985.
21. Lukacs, George, 'Appearance and Essence', in Gaylord C. Roy and Ursula Beitz, ed. *Preserve and Create*, New York, 1973.
22. Mittenzwei, Werner, 'The Brecht-Lukacs Debate' in Gaylord Le Roy and Ursula Beitz, *op. cit.*
23. Misra, P.K., 'From Bride-Price to Dowry' in K. S. Singh, ed. *Economies of the Tribes and Their Transformation*, New Delhi, 1984.
24. Mani, Lata, 'Contentious Traditions : The Debate on Sati in Colonial India', in Kum Kum Sangari and Sudesh Vaid, eds., *Recasting Women : Essays in Colonial History*, Kali For Women, 1989.
25. Mibang, Tamo, 'Indigeneous Faiths and Practices of the Minyongs', in Tanka B. Suba and Karubaki Datta, eds., *Religion and Society in the Himalayas*, New Delhi, 1991.
26. Nash, J. 'A Note on Groom-price', *American Anthropologist*, 1978-80 (1) : 101-108.

27. Ohm Britta, 'Doordarshan : Representing the Nation State', in Christian Brosius and Melissa Butcher, ed., *op. cit*.

28. Patnaik, Arun Kumar, 'Gramsci's Concept of Common - sense', *Economic and Political Weekly* January 30, 1988, PE-2 to PE-10.

29. Panikkar, K.N., 'The Intellectual History of Colonial India : Some Historiographical and Conceptual Questions' in Bhattacharya, Sabyasachi and Romila Thapur, eds., *Situating Indian History*, Delhi, 1986.

30. Padu Gamli, 'Neppe-Nyida', *Arunachal News* April-May 1982.

31. Pandey, Gyanendra, 'Community as History' in Pandey, Gyanendra, *The Construction of Communalism in Colonial in North India*, (Delhi : Oxford University Press, 1944), First Published in 1990.

32. Rukbo, Talom 'Donyi-Poloism : A Religion '*Arunachal News*, July-December 1985, pp. 1-4.

33. Sangma, M.S., 'Attempts to Christianize the People of Arunachal Pradesh by the American Baptist Missionaries (1836-1950), *Proceedings of North-East India History Association*, Pasighat, 1986 (Seventh Session).

34. Sarkar, Jayanta Kumar, 'Development of Identity Consciousness in Arunachal Pradesh', in K. S. Singh, ed. *Tribal Movements In India*, Vol. I, Delhi, 1980.

35. Singh, Mohan, 'Transition from Bride-Price to Dowry : Marriage Payments in a Rural North India Area', *Man in India*, 77 (2 And 3) : June-September 1997.

36. Schlegel, A. and E. Eloul, 'Marriage Transaction : Labour Property, Status', *American Anthropologist*, 1988, 90 (2) : 291-309.

37. Thompson, E. P., 'Folklore, Anthropology and Social History', January 1977, volume iii, Number, 2, INDIAN HISTORY REVIEW, January 1977.

—

38. Tapper, Nancy, 'Direct Exchange and Bride-Price : Alternative Forms in A Complex marriage system', *Man*, Vol. 16, 1981 pp. 387-407.

39. Valeri, Valerio, 'Buying Women but not Selling Them : Gift and Commodity Exchange in Hualu Alliance', *Man*, Vol. 29, No.1 March 1992 pp. 1-26.

40. Williams, Raymond, 'Literature and Sociology', *New Left Review*, May-June, 1971.

Books Cited

1. Aggarwal, Kailash S., ed, *Dynamics of Identity and Inter – group Relations in North-East India*, Indian Institute of Advanced Study, Shimla, 1999.

2. Adorno W. and Max Horkheimer, *Dialectic of Enlightenment*, Tr. John Cumming, NLB, London, 1979.

3. Anderson, Benedict, *Imagined Communities*, Reflections on the origin and spread of Nationalism, Verso, London, 1983.

4. Bhuyan, S.K., *Anglo-Assemese Relations*, 1771-1826, Gauhati, 1949.

5. Brecht, Bertold, Brecht On Theatre, Hill and Wang, 1964.

6. Bourdieu, Pierre, *Outline of a Theory of Practice*, Tr. R. Nice, Cambridge, 1977.

7. Barthes, Roland, *The Pleasure of Text*, Cape, 1978.

8. Bourdieu, Pierre, *Distinction*, Harvard University Press, Cambridge, 1984.

9. Beteille, Andre, *Ideologies And Intellectuals*, New Delhi, 1980.

10. Chaudhury, D.P., *The North-East Frontier of India*, 1865-1914, The Asiatic Society, Kolkata, 1826.

11. Chaudhury, J.N., *Arunachal Through the Ages*, Concept, New Delhi.

12. Chaube, Shibani Kinkar, *Hill Politics in North-East India*, Orient Longman, Mumbai, 1973.

13. Chatterjee, R.K., *Mass Communication* (National Book Trust, India), New Delhi, 1973.

14. Chakravarty, Sumita, *Identity and Authenticity : Nationhood and the Popular Indian Cinema*, 1947-62, Ph.D. Thesis, University of Illinois, Nehru Memorial Centre for Contemporary Studies, Teen Murti House, New Delhi.

15. Chandra, Bipan, *The Rise and Growth of Economic Nationalism*, New Delhi, 1969.

16. Chauhan, Abha, *Tribal Women and Social Change in India*, Etawah, 1990.

17. Dutta Parul and Syed Ishteaque Ahmad, eds. *Arunachal Pradesh*, Volume xiv, Anthropological Survey of India, Kolkata, 1995, General Editor K.S. Singh, *People of India*, Series.

18. Dubey, Sanjay, *Dynamics of Tribal Local Polity and Panchayat Raj in Arunachal Pradesh* (Premier Publishing House, New Delhi, 1998).

19. Elwin, Verrier, *Myths of The Norht-Eastern of India*, North-East Frontier Agency, Shillong, 1958.

20. Elwin, Verrier, *A Philosophy for NEFA*, Shillong, 1964.

21. Elias, Norbert, *The Civilizing Process*, Vol. I. (The History of Manners), Tr. E. Jephcott, New York, Pantheon, 1978.

22. Elwin, Verrier, *Democracy in NEFA*, Shillong, 1965.

23. Foucault, Michel, *Power/Knowledge : Selected Interviews and Other Writing* : 1972-73, Ed, Colin Gordo, *et al.*, New York, 1980.

24. Fost, Howard, *Literature and Reality*, Mumbai, 1953.

25. Fox Ralph, *The Novel and the People*, Moscow, 1956.

26. Forbes, Geraldine, *Women in Modern India*, The New

Cambridge History of India, New Delhi : Cambridge University Press, 1988, Reprint 1999.

27. Gait, E. *A History of Assam*, Kolkata, 1926.
28. Gramsci, Antonio, *Selections From The Prison Note Books*, edited and Translated By Quintin Hoare and Geoffrey Nowell Smith (International Publishers, New York, 1971).
29. Gramsci, Antonio, *Selections From Cultural Writings*, ed. David Forges and Geoffrey Nowel Smith, Translated By William Boel Howel (Harvard University Press, Massachusetts, 1985).
30. Ghosh, Subir, *Mass Communication Today : In the Indian Context, Profile* Publisher, Kolkata.
31. Gopal, S. General Editor, *Selected Works of Jawahar Lal Nehru*, Jawaharlal Nehru Memorial Fund, New Delhi, 1988.
32. Gopal, S. *Jawaharlal Nehru, A Biography*, Vol. 2, 1947-56, Oxford University Press, Delhi, 1983.
33. Goldmann, Lucien, *The Hidden God*, Translated By Philip Thody, London, 1964.
34. Hayes, Douglas E., *Rhetoric and Ritual In Colonial India*, The Shaping of Public Culture in Surat City, 1852-1928, Oxford University Press, 1992.
35. Kakar, Sudhir, *The Inner World : A Psycho-Analytic Study of Childhood and Society in India*, 2nd Edition, (Delhi : Oxford University Press, 1981).
36. Luthra, P. N., *Constitutional and Administrative Growth of The North-East Frontier Agency*, Shillong, 1971.
37. Mackenzie, A., *History of The Relations of the Government with the Hill Tribes of The North-East Frontier of Bengal*, Kolkata, 1884.
38. Mathur, J. C., *New Lamps for Aladdin* (Mass Media In Developing Societies), - Orient Longmans, New Delhi, 1965.

39. Malhan, P. N., *Communication Media : Yesterday, Today and Tomorrow*, (Publication Division, Ministry of Information and Broadcasting, Government of India, New Delhi, 1985).
40. Mitra, A., *Internal Migration and Economic Development in the Hills*, Omson Publications, New Delhi, 1997.
41. Marx, Karl, *German Ideology*, Edition of 1965, London.
42. Marcuse, Herbert, *The Aesthetic Dimension*, Boston, 1978.
43. Machery, Pierre, *A Theory of Literary Production*, Translated from the French By Geoffrey Hall, Routledge and Kegan Paul, London, 1978.
44. Nyori, Tai, *History and Culture of The Adis*, New Delhi, 1993.
45. Poulantzas, N., *State, Power, Socialism*, New Left Books, 1987.
46. Rose Leo and Margaret W. Disher, *The North-Eastern Frontier Agency of India*, Institute of International Studies, University of California, Berkeley, California, 1967.
47. Roy, Sachin, *Aspects of Padam and Minyong Culture*, North-East Frontier Agency, Shillong, 1966.
48. Rabinow, Paul, *French Modern : Norms and Forms of The Social Environment*, Cambridge, Mass, 1989.
49. Roy, N.C. and P.K. Kuri, *A Study of Land Reform in Arunachal Pradesh*, Report of The Project Sponsored By ICSSR, New Delhi.
50. Rustomji, Nari K., *Verrier Elwin and India's North-Eastern Borderlands*, North-Eastern Hill University, Publications, Shillong, 1988.
51. Singh, Chandrika, *Emergence of Arunachal Pradesh as a State*, Delhi, 1989.
52. Stallysbrass Peter and Allon White, *The Politics and Poetics of Transgression*, London, 1986.

53. Singhal Arvind and Everett, M. Rogers, *India's Information Revolution* (Sage, New Delhi, 1989).

54. Storey John, *Cultural Studies and The Study of Popular Culture : Theories and Methods*, Edinburg University Press, Edinburg, 1996.

55. Talukdar, Atual Chandra, *Political Transition in the Grass Roots in Tribal India*, Delhi, 1987.

56. Tambling, Jeremy, *Narrative and Ideology*, Philadelphia, 1991.

57. Thapar, Romila, *Past and Prejudice*, Delhi, 1975.

58. Volosinov. V.N., *Marxism and the Philosophy of Language*, Academic Press, 1973.

59. William Raymond, *Politics and Letters*, NLB, London, 1970.

60. William Raymond, *Keywords*, London, Reprinted ed., 1984.

61. White, Hayden, *Tropics of Discourse : Essays in Cultural Criticism*, Baltimore, 1978.

Index

G

H

I

J

K

L

M

N